Preface

KT-468-866

The intention throughout this study aid is to stimulate and guide, to encourage your involvement in the book, and to develop informed responses and a sure understanding of the main details.

Brodie's Notes provide a clear outline of the play or novel's plot, followed by act, scene, or chapter summaries and/or commentaries. These are designed to emphasize the most important literary and factual details. Poems, stories or non-fiction texts combine brief summary with critical commentary on individual aspects or common features of the genre being examined. Textual notes define what is difficult or obscure and emphasize literary qualities. Revision questions are set at appropriate points to test your ability to appreciate the prescribed book and to write accurately and relevantly about it.

In addition, each of these Notes includes a critical appreciation of the author's art. This covers such major elements as characterization, style, structure, setting and themes. Poems are examined technically – rhyme, rhythm, for instance. In fact, any important aspect of the prescribed work will be evaluated. The aim is to send you back to the text you are studying.

Each study aid concludes with a series of general questions which require a detailed knowledge of the book: some of these questions may invite comparison with other books, some will be suitable for coursework exercises, and some could be adapted to work you are doing on another book or books. Each study aid has been adapted to meet the needs of the current examination requirements. They provide a basic, individual and imaginative response to the work being studied, and it is hoped that they will stimulate you to acquire disciplined reading habits and critical fluency.

Graham Handley 1990

The author and his work

Thomas Stearns Eliot was born in 1888. Originally, the Eliots hailed from the village of East Coker in Somerset. Andrew Eliot emigrated to Boston, Massachusetts, in the seventeenth century and the family remained there for some two hundred years, until the poet's father moved to St Louis, Missouri. T. S. Eliot was born in St Louis and from there he embarked on a brilliant academic career, which took him eventually to Merton College, Oxford (1914) via Harvard and the Sorbonne. In 1915, having decided to settle in England, Eliot married his first wife Vivienne Haigh. In seeking to earn a living, he was briefly a schoolmaster and then in the employ of Lloyds Bank (1919–1922). In 1925 he joined the publishers Faber and Faber as literary editor – this firm published all Eliot's work and he became, eventually, a Director of the establishment.

Eliot began to gain recognition as a poet while he was editor of two literary magazines: *The Egoist* (1917–18) and *The Criterion* (1923–39). It was in *The Criterion* that Eliot published *The Waste Land* – a poem which established his reputation.

In 1927 Eliot became a British Citizen. He was also received into the Church of England, after a long quest to achieve faith in God. Following this conversion, his work became more religious in tone and culminated in his great religious poem *The Four Quartets* (1943).

Once he became recognized as a poet, Eliot enjoyed the friendship of many of the great writers of his time, including Yeats, James Joyce and D. H. Lawrence. He was for a time part of the celebrated 'Bloomsbury' group, of which Virginia Woolf was the leading light. Eliot's first wife died in 1947; he remarried in 1957. Late in his life he received the Nobel Prize for literature and the Order of Merit. He died in 1965.

As well as being one of the major poets of the twentieth century, T. S. Eliot's literary criticism was particularly important in establishing the reputation of John Donne and the 'Metaphysical' poets. He wrote illuminatingly on the drama of Shakespeare and his contemporaries, and also contributed greatly to the appreciation and understanding of Jacobean drama.

All T. S. Eliot's plays are verse-dramas and he was an

Contents

DISCARDED

Page references in these notes are to the Faber and Faber edition of *Murder in the Cathedral* but the notes may be used with any edition of the play important influence upon the re-establishing of verse as a medium for contemporary drama. *Murder in the Cathedral* was the first of his plays, though he had experimented with verse-drama in *Sweeney Agonistes* and *The Rock*.

Murder in the Cathedral was written for the Canterbury Festival of 1935, and designed to be performed in the Chapter House of the Cathedral – close to where Becket was murdered in 1170. The play enjoyed great critical and popular success.

Plot summary

The poor women of Canterbury, who form a Chorus, tell of
the desolation of the people during the seven years that Becket
has been in exile from his diocese. He has quarrelled with
King Henry II and the King has quarrelled with the Pope,
but these antagonisms are great matters, beyond the understanding of humble folk; all they know is that they are miser-
able without the help and protection of their spiritual father.
Three Priests also look forward to the return of Thomas,
which, it seems, is imminent. There is some apparently good
news: Becket has patched up his antagonism with the King.
Even the Messenger, who brings news that Thomas has
landed in England, does not seem hopeful that the reconciliation will be permanent. The Chorus becomes fearful that
Thomas's return will bring strife; they are rebuked by the
Second Priest but, while he is actually speaking, Becket
returns.

As we learn later, the Archbishop's real difficulty is not his
quarrel with the King, which is irremediable, but his failure to
submit his will to the Will of God. The Four Tempters perceive this, and every one of them makes some reference to
Becket's pride, but each has his individual approach. The
First Tempter reminds Becket of the old pleasures he once
enjoyed as the King's favourite. The Second and Third offer
him power, which he may obtain either by once more becoming Chancellor, or by forming an alliance with the barons
against the King. Becket rejects all three temptations without
much difficulty. But the direct temptation to spiritual pride of
the Fourth Tempter, who surprises him, is more powerful.
This Tempter echoes Becket's own innermost thoughts and
desires as he reminds him of the temporal and eternal glories
that await the martyr. Realizing he is prone to spiritual pride,
Becket feels himself trapped: how can he be sure that he is
fulfilling the will of God and not merely pursuing his own
ends?

Becket withdraws momentarily in despair. He returns, de-
termined not to seek the way of martyrdom for personal
glorification – and a new certainty has been born of his
doubts: having wrestled with temptation, he now feels that he

is able to submit himself entirely to the Will of God and accept humbly whatever God may have in store for him. He is aware that this will probably lead to his death.

During the Interlude Becket, with new confidence, explains his position to the audience and to the Chorus, in a sermon preached on Christmas morning. At the conclusion of the sermon he suggests that Canterbury will soon have a new martyr – himself.

The Second Part, like the First, opens with the Chorus; the women now look forward to the work of a new year but they dread an unknown, inevitable doom that is soon to come. Following the Chorus, the Priests tell of the feast days that succeed Christmas Day; they have just reached the fourth day – which, as yet, celebrates no saint – when the four Knights enter and demand to see the Archbishop. Becket comes to them and the Knights accuse him of ingratitude and dis-loyalty to the King; they refer particularly to his action in suspending the Bishops, who crowned the King's son; then, with further threats, they depart.

The Chorus now comments upon the action: evil is abroad; the whole world is evil; everything in it is unnatural and horrible. Becket tries to comfort the women but his priests run in and drag him off to find safety in the Cathedral. They try to persuade him also to bar the doors but Becket demands that they be kept open. The Four Knights burst in and kill Becket on the chancel steps.

After another Chorus speech, Reginald Fitz Urse (First Knight) assumes the manner of an after-dinner chairman speaker, as does de Traci (Third Knight), whom he now introduces; followed by de Morville (Second Knight) and Brito (Fourth Knight). All four offer excuses for their action and urge that the people disperse quietly. As the Knights leave, the priests gradually come to the realization that God has given 'another Saint to Canterbury', and with a new 'Te Deum', the play ends.

Historical background

Thomas à Becket was born in Cheapside in 1118. The son of a London merchant, he came from Norman stock. He was edu-cated at Merton Priory, eventually rounding off his education in the schools of theology in Paris. A natural scholar, he was none the less noted for his skill at the joust and on the dance-floor. He distinguished himself in the Toulouse Campaign of 1159–60, defeating a French knight in single combat. In 1141, he became the protégé of Theobald, Archbishop of Canterbury. Becket's success in various ecclesiastical diplomatic endeavours brought him to the notice of Henry II and, at the age of 36, he was made Chancellor of England. He had formed a deep friendship with the King.

Theobald died and was succeeded by Becket as Archbishop of Canterbury; at first, by special dispensation from the Pope, he was permitted to hold the offices of Chancellor and Archbishop. In his personal life, however, Becket changed: he became an ascetic, shunning worldliness – he resigned the chancellorship, to the great disappointment of his friend the King. Bitter disputes arose between the two men.

The fundamental cause of dissension concerned the relationship between Church and State. The King was desirous of reducing the power of the clergy; Becket emphatically opposed any diminution of ecclesiastical power. The chief point at issue was the question of the 'criminous clerks': the King wished that clergy who committed criminal offences should face trial in civil courts, whereas Becket insisted that they could only be tried by ecclesiastical courts – by tradition, no unsanctified person had the right to apprehend an ordained and consecrated priest. The King attempted to regularize the relationship between Church and State, in this and similar matters, by drawing up the Constitutions of Clarendon (1164). This document was sent to Becket for his consideration: he threw it out. The King, angered, lost patience. Charges were laid that Becket had misappropriated funds while he was Chancellor; feeling himself threatened, he fled to France. The King declared all Becket's goods forfeit.

Becket spent nearly seven years on the Continent. Both men sought the support of the Pope for their cause. Eventually matters came to a head when Henry, believing the Pope too insecure to oppose him, attempted to make firm the claim of his son to succeed him to the throne, by having him crowned – while Henry was, of course, still alive! This procedure was unprecedented in English Law. Its legality was further in doubt because the 'coronation' was carried out by the Archbishop of York, supported by the Bishops of London and Salisbury. Thus the only person who could lawfully carry out the coronation, the exiled Becket, was effectively bypassed. This was an insult that neither Pope nor Archbishop of Canterbury could tolerate. Papal letters were dispatched to Becket, suspending the offending bishops. Various attempts at reconciliation failed (notably at Montmirail). The order excommunicating the bishops was published by Becket on 1 December. The next day, Becket returned to England. In his Christmas sermon he roundly condemned those who had appropriated his property during his absence.

On hearing that his bishops had been excommunicated, Henry, who was still in France, is alleged to have made his famous remark: 'Will no man rid me of this turbulent priest?' Acting upon the angry words of their King, four knights (Fitz Urse, de Morville, de Traci and Brito) set out for Canterbury. They murdered Becket on the chancel steps of the cathedral – the date was 29 December 1170.

Setting

Although the play draws upon historical sources it is not in the accepted sense a 'history play'. The background of events surrounding the murder of Becket in 1170 is alluded to, but not chronicled on stage. Eliot's primary interest is focused on the theological and philosophical implications of the martyrdom. The drama centres on Becket's soul and the political drama is only of interest in so far as it has a bearing upon Becket's relationship with God.

The everyday concerns of life as depicted by the Chorus are appropriate to the play's time-setting, and such circumstances as are revealed surrounding the actual murder are accurate. The text of Becket's sermon is the one he used when he preached for the last time in the Cathedral.

The play is suddenly, and for dramatic effect, wrenched into our own times when the Knights address the audience towards the end of the play – but this is primarily the result of the language they employ.

Section summaries, critical commentary, textual notes and revision questions

Part 1

Pages 11–13 The Chorus

The poor women of Canterbury, who comprise the Chorus, gather in a mood of fear and anxiety outside Canterbury Cathedral. They do not know why they seek the shelter of the cathedral, except that they seem compelled to watch and witness some dreadful occurrence. The New Year is upon them but they do not welcome it – they see it merely as another moment in an unending seasonal cycle. Essentially, the women seek a quiet life, yet they sense that the quietude and certainties of seasonal drudgery are about to be shattered by the arrival of their Archbishop, Thomas, who has been exiled in France for seven years.

Eliot derives the Chorus from Greek Drama, where according to that tradition it observes and comments upon the action of the play. As we shall see, the Chorus do not remain passive – they become progressively (and against their will) involved in the events they witness. In a sense, the Chorus stands for the common people of all times who find themselves caught up in great moments of history.

The verse in this passage betokens desolation and lack of a sense of purpose: the poor women reveal life without meaning, they are mere slaves to the seasons and devoid of any spiritual dimension to their lives. They sense that something terrible is about to happen and they lack the inner resources to cope with it. They are aware that they are victims of baronial oppression and they are content merely to be left alone. Yet, despite appearances, the poor women, on an instinctive level, perceive their need for spiritual leadership – thus they gather near the cathedral. Also instinctively, they perceive that the arrival of Thomas threatens their way of life – in this they are correct, but they are wrong to suppose that he betokens some new malady. The advent of a saint and martyr is to breathe new life into the people – but this remains in the future.

Thus, at the opening of the play the audience finds itself provided with some information, but at this stage, more importantly, it is introduced to a mood of despair, and inevitably it catches something of the Chorus's sense of foreboding – suspense is aroused.

knowledge of safety Traditionally the sanctuary of a cathedral provided a place of refuge for the pursued and the persecuted.

presage Premonition, ill-omen.

golden October ... sombre November The first of the play's many references to the seasons. Here the imagery suggests the fading of light and beauty and the onset of darkness – appropriate, if misguided, to the present mood of the Chorus. Eliot intends that we should share the mood at this point, just as we share the spiritual light and insight at the end of the play.

stretches hand ... fire Recalls St Peter, who denied Christ (Mark, 14, 66–68). Eliot intends that we should ask the question: will Thomas, when his hour of trial comes, 'deny his Master'?

All Hallows All Saints Day (1 November). Eliot keeps the notion of sainthood firmly before the audience.

Seven years. .. The rhythm alters, becoming more regular, shifting from the earlier wailing lament. Becket left England for France in 1164, it is now 1170.

Winter ... death from the sea Anticipates the imminent arrival of Thomas, who is shortly to die at the hands of the Four Knights.

Destiny waits in the hand of God The predestined course of events is perceived to be different from that prescribed by the politician. The Divine Plan triumphs in the play ... at the expense of that of those who practise statecraft (and treachery) in the material world.

shaft of sunlight The imagery suggests a moment of insight or intuition in the midst of obscurity i.e. sunlight breaking through clouds.

happy December Happy because it celebrates the birth of Christ – and, as we shall see, the martyrdom and subsequent sainthood of Thomas.

litter of scorn Refers to Christ's humble birthplace and to the scorn he endured on the Cross. A parallel is frequently suggested between the Crucifixion and the martyrdom of Thomas. From the agony of death new life comes; in seasonal terms, the old year dies and the New Year arrives.

Pages 13–16 The Three Priests and the Messenger

The seven years since the departure of Thomas have been a time of turmoil, which derives from the conflict between Church and State, Thomas and Henry II. The Third Priest concludes that all politics is essentially violence, graft and treachery. There seems no end to this dismal state of affairs. A messenger arrives with the news that Thomas is at hand. Anxiously, the priests enquire if the hostility between King and Archbishop is at an end. The Third Priest is pessimistic. The Messenger replies that Thomas has been welcomed by the common people but there is no real peace between Henry and his Archbishop; it is merely a papering-over of the cracks.

The First Priest fears for the Church and State; Thomas is perceived as being possessed by pride, which precludes any reconciliation with the King. The Second Priest draws some comfort from the fact of Thomas's return – at least they may look forward to some leadership. The Third Priest is fatalistic: life in this world can never bring fulfilment.

The Priests, more educated and aware of the political situation between Church and State, are able to provide the audience with some necessary historical information. Underlying their knowledge is the same anxiety about the future and the same basic need for spiritual sustenance. The arrival of the Messenger (again borrowed from Greek Drama, where action takes place off-stage) heightens the dramatic tension by describing the arrival of Thomas; here there are some unmistakable echoes of Christ's arrival in Jerusalem. The fact that the peace is unreal emphasizes that matters between the King and Thomas are irreconcilable, and the outcome will probably have to be the death of Thomas. The First Priest's admonitions about Becket's pride serve to introduce a subject that is to be presented by the Fourth Tempter. The Second Priest displays a facile but understandable optimism.

For all their anxiety about the political situation, the Priests do not appear so lost and apathetic as the Chorus – they need their Archbishop, but their need is not nearly so profound. For good or ill, one feels that the Priests can cope; perhaps secure in their religion, they (notably the Third Priest) are adjusted to the chance and change of the temporal world.

malversation Misappropriation of money.
their friend Emphasizes Becket's sympathy for the common people.
two proud men The similarity between Henry II and Becket is indicated.
the hammer and the anvil An image suggesting irresistible force and immovable object.

full assurance ... Rome Is Becket secure in his reconciliation with the King, or does he only have the assurance of the Pope's support – i.e. is he secure temporally as well as spiritually?

relic Anticipates Becket's elevation to sainthood! This passage echoes the description in Mark Chapter 11 of Christ's entry into Jerusalem.

kiss of peace Symbol of the King's forgiveness – denied by Henry to Becket.

pretensions strongly held beliefs, claims

in this life Becket perceives that their conflict will never be settled – and maybe anticipates his own death.

Pages 17–21 The Chorus

Still seeking to be left alone to pursue their lives without disturbance, The Chorus urges that Thomas should leave immediately and return to France. Fear and a sense of doom predominate – they do not wish to be drawn into any action; they wish to remain apart from what they sense fate has in store. The Second Priest rudely interrupts them and demands their silence; he then calls (insensitively) upon them to give the Archbishop a hearty welcome.

The impassioned response of the Chorus contrasts vividly with the settled rhythms of the Third Priest's preceding utterance. The Chorus then speaks with great regularity, as it relates the small happinesses and routine afflictions of everyday life: 'living and partly living'. But they sense that this monotony is about to be shattered by the return of Thomas, and they return to their insistence that they be left alone. The Chorus expresses, implicitly, a deep fear of change: they dread the catastrophe that they sense is coming upon them. They do not, at this stage, appreciate that the pain may be a prelude to a rebirth. They dread the death of the old world and do not entertain the possibilities of the new. They are without faith.

pride ... virtues A worldly-wise comment which anticipates the Fourth Tempter.

temporal devolution i.e. the power which came to him from the Chancellorship.

God alone Implies that Becket always (and unreasonably) gave primacy to his spiritual power – as Archbishop.

our lord A possible ambiguity – referring not only to Becket but also to Christ.

let the wheel turn Refers to the 'Wheel of Fortune'. Becket uses the image of a wheel later in the play.

Until the grinders cease An image drawn from Ecclesiastes 12, 3–4 – implying the onset of tribulation.

continuing city See Hebrews 13, 14 – a passage that stresses the transitoriness of earthly things.

late late ... too late Eliot relies here and elsewhere in the speech upon repetition to convey the urgency of their request.

death into Canterbury True, but they do not perceive that the death (of Thomas) is to give them rebirth and renewal of spirit.

Living and partly living One of the most evocative phrases of the play, which expresses both the humdrum nature of the women's everyday lives and the lives of all who live without a spiritual dimension.

kept the feasts ... masses i.e. 'gone through the motions' of religion.

birth and death ... apart They confess here to be unable to make the connection – this is their blindness, which accentuates their fear.

We Note the emphatic placing of this word, followed by a long pause. In harping on the Chorus's own fear and eagerness to be left alone, they force us to confront their moral cowardice.

brains ... onion A particularly vivid image – appropriate to humble working-women.

unaffrayed A word invented by Eliot: possibly implied is that the women do not want to be involved in any 'affray' – an 'affray' they dimly sense will come to pass. Also, the word carries the obvious sense, 'unafraid'.

Croaking like frogs A dismissive simile that emphasizes the gulf in feeling between priest and flock.

Pages 21–43 Thomas and The Four Tempters

Thomas enters and tells the Priests of his narrow escape on landing at Sandwich; he is under no illusion, however, and foresees that he will not ultimately escape his enemies, who have sworn to kill him.

The First Tempter is a voice from Thomas's past, who invites him to become reconciled with the King and recapture the old days of sensuous delight and happiness. Thomas advises this Tempter to think of penitence. Clearly Thomas feels no allure from this quarter: this world is dead to him. The Second Tempter offers Thomas the temptation to return to the chancellorship and enjoy the fruits of power under the King. The appeal is given added subtlety by the possibility of using power to help the poor and to maintain order in the kingdom. Once again, Thomas resists without difficulty; clearly, earthly power holds no temptation for the Archbishop. He also maintains his right to excommunicate the Bishops of Salisbury, London and York.

The Third Tempter suggests that Thomas lend his authority to the cause of liberty; nationalism; to defeat the King with the blessing of the Church; patriotism before loyalty to the monarch. Again, Thomas rebuffs the temptation: he will have nothing to do with 'causes' that are not God's causes and he will certainly not seek to destroy the King's authority, which he helped to establish. Thomas did not expect the Fourth Tempter, and his temptation is the most telling of all. Thomas is invited to seek the way of the martyr so that he may attain sainthood – thus he is invited to achieve supreme glory and exercise power from the tomb. Thomas is deeply affected by this temptation – in effect, he is being tempted by that which, by his own admission, he desires.

Thomas's first words betoken concern for the poor women, and offer some rebuke to the Second Priest. He then launches into a difficult speech, which seems to indicate that the Chorus is possessed of a knowledge denied to the priest. The paradoxes reveal an understanding that life must involve both action and suffering (patiently accepting the Will of God) – a seeming contradiction – and that by seeking both to act and to suffer, the Divine pattern may be carried forward. Martyrdom is a case in point: it is clearly a suffering, yet if it be willed then the martyr seems to court damnation in the form of spiritual pride. Somehow the act of willing martyrdom must needs be brought together with the suffering. As yet, for Becket, there seems to be no way out of this dilemma; no possibility of harmonizing with the Divine pattern.

The Tempters are representative of aspects of Becket's character. There is a natural temptation to leave well alone and to return to the sensual ways of his youth. Thomas resists this aspect of his nature with relative ease. Likewise, Thomas may be conceived to be seeking a return to the office of Chancellor – this temptation, too, is easily resisted. Significantly, both Tempters so far have alluded to Thomas's pride – the Second Tempter is specific: 'Your spiritual power is earthly perdition.' The Third Tempter again suggests that Thomas exerts earthly power – this time in the interest of the common Englishman against a repressive King. All three

Tempters present Thomas with ways out of his present situation. If we interpret the allegory, we can see that it is important for the development of Thomas that he understands his own natural tendencies – and is able to resist. There is an obvious parallel with Christ's temptation in the wilderness.

The Fourth Tempter takes Thomas by surprise and voices a temptation, which, until now Thomas has been unwilling to acknowledge. Certainly, the temptation put before him is more difficult to resist. Briefly, in this instance, Thomas is invited to seek the way of the martyr and thus achieve an eternal glory – ruling from beyond the grave. Thomas is thus placed in an impossible dilemma: the earlier Tempters offered fulfilment of earthly hopes and desires – the way to eternal damnation. The Fourth Tempter, in offering the fulfilment of eternal glory, is in fact offering Thomas damnation too – this time for the sin of pride.

know and do not know These words are echoed by Thomas later in this episode.

agent The person who acts, does something.

patient The person who suffers, is acted upon.

the pattern i.e. the Divine Plan.

chill off ... December The priest's good-hearted, fussy concern contrasts with the real needs of Thomas – spiritual, rather than physical, well-being.

I am ... grateful Thomas's courtesy is an endearing characteristic.

bishops Henry II, contrary to the practice in England, and in order to secure the succession, had his son crowned during his own lifetime. Thomas, as Archbishop of Canterbury, refused to officiate at this illegal coronation. The coronation was nevertheless carried out by York, London and Salisbury – the 'rebellious bishops'.

Broc ... Kent Enemies of Becket. Brock is said to have housed the Knights before and after Becket's murder.

John, the Dean of Salisbury One of Becket's few ecclesiastical friends.

hungry hawk An image suggesting the imminence of sudden death.

shadows Refers to the temptations which he is to undergo.

the interval Becket regards the time spent awaiting the end as more onerous than the catastrophe itself. Again, probably refers to the period of temptation.

prepare i.e. are a time of preparation for the end (his death).

acrimony bitterness.

gravity . . . levity The casual rhyming creates an insinuating fluidity in the Tempter's speech. Cf. 'amity . . . laity . . . gaiety'.

gay Tom Refers to the worldliness and ease of Becket's youth.

summer's over Summer is indeed over, as the Chorus has constantly reminded us.

viols Stringed instruments, akin to violins.

the wheel . . . turns The same seasons, experiences and situations constantly recur – as part of the cycle of time. From the perspective of humankind, this conveys the feeling of being in a world in which nothing new happens – the future is merely a re-enactment of things that have occurred in the past. Only a fool believes that he is really in control of his life and events; to escape the feeling of being on Time's treadmill man needs to 'sever the cord, shed the scale' – an image of renewal in a spiritual sense.

higher vices i.e. worldly ambitions and spiritual pride. Note the facile rhymes in this speech which emphasize the triviality of the Tempter's point of view. This is a repetition of his opening speech – he has got nowhere with Thomas and is left to repeat himself.

The impossible . . . temptation Expresses the fact that he sometimes wishes he could return to his 'springtime fancy', even though he knows it to be impossible.

mind . . . present Thomas understands the temptation to live in the past, and its destructiveness of the present.

Your Lordship . . . Note the greater formality of this opening when compared with that of the First Tempter.

Clarendon . . . Maine All places where Becket met with Henry. At Clarendon Becket and Henry patched up differences about who was to have the jurisdiction over 'criminous' clergy: the Church Courts or Civil Courts. At Northampton, Becket was called before the King to account for some alleged financial mishandling (Becket was Chancellor). At Montmirail, Henry and Becket finally parted – after declaring an uneasy truce over their differences.

templed tomb Contrasts with the 'jewelled shrine' (symbolizing 'eternal glory') offered by the Fourth Tempter.

protect the poor Obviously would have attraction for Becket, who always shows sympathy with the poor. The temptation is to use power to the material benefit of mankind.

thrive on earth Becket is not interested in Marxism! Man does not live by bread alone.

excommunication Becket had excommunicated the bishops for their involvement in the coronation of Henry's son. Throughout this temptation, Becket refuses to compromise.

intelligent self-interest A phrase which gives away the truth underlying the Tempter's smooth words. Becket will not compromise his 'self'.

curbing ... privilege Becket forced the barons to give up some of their power, thus earning their hatred.

keep the keys A reference to the keys of the Kingdom, granted to the first Pope and founder of the Church – St Peter. Becket will keep this power, which he derives from St Peter. In particular, it may refer to the power to excommunicate.

soars sunward ... An image drawn from falconry. This Tempter, like his predecessor, had tempted Thomas to seek reconciliation with the King, and to subordinate himself to the King's wishes. At this point the Tempter realizes that such temptations are not likely to be influential with Thomas, and therefore appears content to leave him to the more heinous sin of spiritual pride.

... Temporal power ... In rejecting the temptation, Thomas none the less reveals that it had some appeal for him. This is, of course, true of all the temptations – or they would not be temptations, and the episode would lose any dramatic force.

controlled by the order of God God must underpin all material, worldly affairs. A world without God is fatally flawed. The exercise of temporal power can only temporarily arrest the progress of disorder.

I am no trifler ... politician Note the crudity of diction and clipped rhythms of this Tempter's speech – he is representative of the baronial classes, who stayed away from court and believed that they held the country together ('country-keeping' in both senses of the word).

Proceed straight forward Becket assumes an ironic tone – he realizes that such a claim to be 'straightforward' is often a prelude to crookedness.

Purpose is plain Note the dropping of the articles in this speech – it has a certain rough muscularity and directness of tone, but, as Thomas points out, is notably evasive when it comes to particularities.

hungry sons Henry II's sons were quarrelling over lands.

Angevin Henry II was the son of Henry of Anjou.

Church favour Becket is here being asked to compromise the Church – by lending its authority to rebellion.

liberty Like the appeal to patriotism, the appeal to liberty is suspicious.

king's ... bishop's ... baron's Indicative of the power struggle in England at the time. Who was to have jurisdiction?

constellation Star in the heavens – i.e. ruler, implicitly Becket himself.

tilt-yard Becket was expert at the joust in his earlier days.

wolves The image reveals that Becket perceives the true nature of the Tempter.

To make, then break The temptation to break the very laws which he had established.

Samson in Gaza Samson in bringing down the temple upon the Philistines committed an act of self-destruction. To take the Third Tempter's course, Thomas understands, would be similarly self-destructive. But he would merely destroy himself – unlike Samson, who destroyed the Philistines as well.

Well done Ingratiating, suspect and somewhat patronizing.

Who are you? This is the one temptation that Thomas does not initially recognize or expect. It will be harder to deal with.

precede expectation Come before I am expected.

I do not need a name Betokens the fact that the temptation is in Thomas's own heart – in a sense, its name is 'Thomas'. All the other temptations were external, temporal; recognizable and thus easier to conquer.

Fare forward to the end The temptation is to do what Thomas has already decided to do. Significantly, the Tempter goes on to quote words that Thomas himself has recently used. Tempter, temptation and Thomas are one entity.

This is the course of temporal power It is noteworthy that this Tempter, like the Second and the Third, dismisses the arguments of his predecessor.

skein The thread, or yarn in a coil.

but for one Enigmatic: it might mean God or alternatively the Devil. Christ was offered supreme power in the wilderness, provided that he would grant supremacy to the Devil. In either case, the temptation to exalt himself implies damnation, and thus is essentially demonic.

Saint and Martyr In fact, incompatible with self-glorification – in life or after death.

pilgrims, standing in line Becket's tomb did become an object of veneration.

in another place Hell.

You have also thought... The Fourth Tempter's speech here outlines what is to come to pass: the shrine was pillaged at the Reformation and the whole notion of sainthood was to become devalued by Protestant England. In later years, Becket was to become a mere historical figure – a subject of debate among historians. The Tempter is thus in tune with 'modern' attitudes to Thomas. It is ironical that many of the audience at Eliot's play would find themselves caricatured in the last lines of this speech. Later, in the mouth of Becket himself, Eliot is to answer the modernistic view of sainthood and martyrdom – at the end of Part 1. It may seem odd that the Tempter offers

Thomas, on the one hand, eternal glory, only to dismiss it in
this speech.

no enduring crown The Tempter's efforts have had their effect.
Thomas has been offered eternal glory through martyrdom, thus
leading him to damnation. Then in snatching it away, the
Tempter leaves Thomas with nothing but despair – again he is
damned.

Can sinful ... by more sinful? Thomas's situation
encapsulated: if he drives out the sinful pride for worldly ease
and advancement offered by the first three Tempters, he is
confronted by the greater sin of spiritual pride implicit in
seeking sainthood through martyrdom. Ironically, if he rejects
the desire for sainthood he is left with the even greater sin of
despair.

Can I neither ... perdition If he acts in the world to further his
ambition he is damned, if he suffers and becomes a martyr he is
damned too.

You know and do not know The Tempter leaves Thomas still
confronting his dilemma. It is a subtle touch, emphasizing the
identity of view between Thomas and the Fourth Tempter, that
the Tempter should use Thomas's own words (see page 22 of
the play). At this point, Thomas seems no further forward – the
Tempters have been materializations of his inner debate.

Pages 43–48 The Chorus, Priests, Tempters, Thomas

The Chorus speaks of restlessness; there is a sense of oppression and imminent but ill-defined evil. The Tempters join
forces and stress the futility of life's achievements. The Priests
urge passivity and compromise. Next, Chorus, Priests and
Tempters, speaking alternately, tell of the impossibility of
avoiding death, which may arrive suddenly and unexpectedly.
After the Chorus has once more bewailed the hardships of
their lives, they launch into a lamentation that tells of their
feeling that God has deserted them, and culminates in an
urgent appeal to Thomas to save himself. Part One ends with
Thomas now pronouncing that he feels his way to be clear; he
reviews briefly the temptations he has undergone. At the end
of his speech he commits himself into the hands of his 'good
Angel'.

The speech of the Chorus, which begins this episode, contains imagery that betokens dissolution and decay. The
Tempters join in with a 'list' of images that convey the sense
that man's life is nothing but empty show and a series of

disappointments – it flares briefly, perhaps, like the Catherine wheel, only to fizzle out into darkness. Man is obstinate, blind and bent on self-destruction. After briefly urging a 'laissez-faire' policy, the Priests join the Chorus and the Tempters: the imagery darkens still further, suggesting menace, animality and death. There is an appreciable oppressiveness, which is enhanced by the Chorus's images of life being meaningless and subject to the onset of violent death. Rhythmically, the Chorus ends on a wailingly urgent plea that Thomas save himself. The effect of all this is to mirror the feeling of despair with which the previous episode ended.

A new Thomas has been born from the travail and despair that threatened to overwhelm him. The resolution and calm of Thomas's speech contrast with the words of the Chorus that precede it. The pattern is apparent and universal: from the inner chaos and inertia that threatened Thomas, has been born a harmony of self and sense of purpose: he now knows that his way is clear. By the end of the play his inspiration will have brought harmony and inner peace to the Chorus. In seasonal terms, the harshness of winter will have given way to hope of spring.

Thomas's intervention here is dramatically satisfying. It reveals to us that the Tempters and the Chorus have played their part in his renewal. The Tempters, unwitting agents of God, have tested the strength of Thomas's resolve and, more importantly, have forced him to examine his conscience in the face of what lies before him. It is now clear to Thomas that the way of the martyr, if it is to avoid the deadly sin of spiritual pride, must involve the submission of self to the Divine Will – in this way, it is, in a sense, not a personal decision. Thus is resolved his dilemma of action and suffering: to submit oneself to God is both to act and to suffer. The Chorus too has played its part: their need, so frequently expressed, has impinged upon Thomas so that he acts on their behalf – their restoration of faith follows hard upon his own. Thus the Church is renewed through the blood of its martyrs.

In a very telling moment, at the end of his speech, Thomas turns and addresses the audience of the play – its complacency is jolted. The first three 'yous' probably refer to the Chorus, the Priests and the Tempters, but the '. . . So must you' seems directed at *us* – we are not exculpated from the sacrilege and wrong that is about to take place at the murder of Thomas. It is a profound irony, and mystery (in the religious sense), that from the midst of evil God brings forth good. At the moment of suffering and death (like Christ) Thomas redeems and atones for the evil that destroys him.

parturition The act of bringing forth, giving birth. The Chorus senses the unleashing of a great evil upon the earth. In particular, this must refer to the act of murder.

Catherine wheel ... Essay ... decoration ... The images here not only suggest that transitoriness of earthly joys and achievements, but also stress man's childishness and the fragility of his illusions. There may also be a relevant irony in that the heroic martyrdom of St Catherine is 'celebrated' by a cheap firework.

Chorus, Priests *and* Tempters Eliot here 'borrows' a device from Greek drama: stichomythia – dialogue in which alternate speakers utter single lines, each one 'capping' his predecessor.

owl that calls ... cold in his groin The images here suggest the imminence of death. They are very sinister.

torn girl ... mill-stream Imagery suggesting the routines of life, interrupted by acts of great violence.

God is leaving us ... death Note the prevailing feeling of despair in these lines; the Chorus may be seen as enacting not only its own despair but also the hopelessness that has recently been shown by Thomas.

Puss-purr ... hyaena ... dark air Highly onomatopoeic lines. Animal imagery reflects the bestial act of murder.

save us save us Increasing desperation and panic.

Now is my way Note the sudden easing of the tension. Thomas begins with words of almost conversational ease.

To do ... wrong reason An important idea in the play. This was the essence of the Fourth Tempter's temptation. It has been perceived and conquered.

venial Venial sin may be more easily pardoned than mortal. It has 'natural vigour' in so far as it seems easy and natural. Unfortunately venial sin often leads to mortal sin. But for Thomas the natural vigour of his early sins remained venial, and he avoided 'advancing' to the mortal variety.

Sin grows with doing good A seeming paradox – but easily testable in experience. Goodness must be based upon spiritual values.

Servant of God ... greater sin i.e. spiritual pride, which Thomas faced in the shape of the Fourth Tempter.

most of you ... futility Eliot (through Becket) addressed a secular age. It is also the view of the Fourth Knight.

strangest consequence ... cause The consequence of the act of

evil (murder) will be the renewal of faith in all who witness it –
and possibly in ourselves, who witness it in this play.

no longer act or suffer The contraries have been reconciled for
Becket by surrendering himself to the design of God. He is at
peace.

Pages 51–54 The Interlude

Thomas preaches in Canterbury Cathedral on Christmas
morning, 1170. His sermon is closely and clearly argued: he
begins with an analysis of the deep meaning of the Mass,
which enacts the Passion and Death of Our Lord, yet at the
same time is a celebration of His birth. An occasion, therefore,
of simultaneous mourning and rejoicing – a Christian Mystery, or paradox. The same may be said of martyrdom –
again, a notion that Thomas analyses in some detail. He
concludes with an injunction that his hearers keep his words
in their hearts because he believes that this will be the last
occasion on which he will preach to them.

Such is the lucidity of Eliot's prose that commentary is
almost superfluous. The idea that Thomas should preach a
sermon is simple but effective: it enables Thomas to address
his congregation as well as the audience of the play (his larger
congregation). Drama, for the Greeks, was a religious experience, which the audience shared with the actors. This idea is
neatly and naturally given modern equivalence at this point
by the sermon. The prose serves to elucidate the decision of
Thomas and to lend variety to the exposition of the themes
that have hitherto been expressed in verse.

Ideas, which are central to an understanding of the play,
are laid before us. Thomas explains the Christian understanding of 'peace'. It is clear from what Thomas says that man
should not look for peace in the customary sense of the word;
the Christian peace is the peace that comes from inner
harmony with the Will of God – it is this peace that enables Thomas to face his own death and come to terms with
martyrdom. This is the peace the Chorus may expect to
achieve through the medium of the martyrdom and sainthood
of Thomas, and it will enable the humble women of Canterbury to endure patiently the vicissitudes of living. In his consideration of martyrdom, Thomas reveals that (like the Mass
on Christmas morning) it may be regarded as an occasion for

both rejoicing and mourning. Mourning it must be, for we lament that we are deprived of a good man by the sins of the world, which lead to his martyrdom; but it is most significantly an occasion for rejoicing, in that the Will of God has been enacted and 'another soul is numbered among the saints in Heaven, for the glory of God and the salvation of men.' Thus Christian martyrdom is a means whereby man may return to the way of God – in this sense, it stands as an example of faith even unto death. There is, of course, an inescapable parallel with the Crucifixion. In speaking of martyrdom, Thomas emphasizes that it is never an accident and always the design of God; it is never the will of the martyr himself. Thus Thomas underlines the resolution of the dilemma, which had faced him earlier in the play.

The sermon ends on a quietly personal note, as Thomas bids farewell to his congregation. It has been a moment of remarkable impact in the drama.

Mass The most important Christian act of worship: a celebration of the Lord's Supper.
oblation and satisfaction These words appear in The Book of Common Prayer. 'Oblation' is an offering to God.
War and the fear of War Words applicable to Thomas's audience and to all peoples of all times.
My peace ... I give unto you John 14, 27. Words spoken by Christ just prior to His Crucifixion.
Stephen The first Christian martyr, who was stoned to death in the presence of Saul of Tarsus, who later became St Paul. Stephen's martyrdom is celebrated on the day after Christmas.
Elphege St Elphege (Aelfeah), Archbishop of Canterbury (1006–12). He was murdered by the Danes for his refusal to pay ransom money.

Revision questions on Part 1 and the Interlude

1 Discuss the impact of the first speech of the Chorus. What impressions does it leave with you concerning their state of mind?
2 Do you think that the Three Priests are differentiated in character and attitude? Illustrate your answer by means of examples.
3 Show how Eliot prepares his audience for the arrival of Thomas. What are the first impressions he creates?

4 Contrast the attitudes of the Priests and the Chorus with respect to the imminent return of Thomas.

5 Why does the Chorus wish to be left alone to pursue its way of life?

6 Indicate the substance of the four temptations. Explain the particular subtlety of the Fourth Tempter.

7 'There is insufficient dramatic interest to sustain our involvement in the play.' Support or refute this remark with reference to Part 1 of the play.

8 Show how the attitude of the Chorus towards Becket's return changes during Part 1 of the play.

9 Summarize Becket's Christmas Morning sermon. What contribution do you think that it makes to the play?

10 How far is the sermon a help towards our understanding of the play?

Part 2

Pages 57–61 The Chorus, the three Priests

The Chorus waits, sensing that something is about to happen. They look forward to spring, but they are oppressed by the winter, and a feeling that the onset of spring is about to cover up some great wrong. They are apprehensive. The Three Priests denote the passion of time by chanting passages from the Epistles appropriate to the saints' days that follow Christmas. They reach the fourth day, when they are interrupted by the Four Knights.

The bird images reflect the mood of the Chorus and the play. They listen for the bird from the south, which denotes the approach of spring, but they hear only the cry of the sea-bird, which has been driven in from the sea – a reflection of their own need for shelter. For the Chorus, spring is still a time more associated with death than with birth. This winter is worse than usual: the day is longer and darker. More bird imagery (the crow and the owl) suggest the proximity of death. Despite all this there is a hint of hope – the winter, for all its harshness, is seen as a time of cleansing and there is a sense of life and colour in the images of the frolicsome children and the leaves sprouting from the trees.

Thus, despite the abiding sense of death, fear and anticipation, at a deeper level there may just be something to be hoped for. This is appropriate mood-painting, as we approach the murder of Thomas.

The Introits chanted by the Priests emphasize the liturgical aspect of the play. It is a clever device to mark the passage of time in this way – after the scattered apprehensions of the Chorus, we perceive a new sense of order: the fourth day after Christmas still awaits its saint, but the pattern of days is established, and this day will soon have its saint, as Thomas takes his place within the Divine pattern of events.

The peace of this world ... God The Chorus here echoes the thought expressed earlier by Thomas in his sermon.
death in the Lord Refers to the deaths of Christ and of martyrs.
leaf ... elder ... children Images which suggest spring and rebirth.

Princess moreover did sit See Psalm 119,23 and Mark, 14,56. These verses are particularly appropriate to Thomas, who was spoken against by 'Princes' (the King) and many 'bore false witness' against him.

Introit An anthem, sung at the beginning of the Mass, as the priest approaches the altar.

In the midst of the congregation ... mouth See Psalm 22,22. Again appropriate to Thomas.

Holy Innocents Children slaughtered by Herod, in the hope of thus killing Jesus. See Matthew 2,16.

Out of the mouths of very babes Psalm 8,2. This verse has a relevance to the Chorus, who may themselves be thought of as Holy Innocents.

They sung ... song See Psalm 96,1. Again relevant to the Chorus.

The blood of thy saints See Psalm 79,2–3.

No man to bury them See Psalm 79,3.

Avenge ... saints Deuteronomy, 22,43.

In Rama See Matthew 2,18.

Rejoice ... holy See Psalm 42,4.

He lays ... sheep See John 10,14–15.

All these references have an obvious relevance to the play at this point.

Today, what is today? This repeated rhetorical question increases the dramatic tension and suggests that the Priests are once again caught up in the endless passage of time.

Every day ... now and here Expresses the idea that time and eternity cohere in the present. The 'critical moment', when time and eternity meet is forever now. This paradox is evidenced by the moment of martyrdom, which occurs in time yet is for all time – eternity.

retrospection Looking back in time.

sordid particulars An appropriate introduction to the Four Knights.

Pages 61–72 The Three Knights, the Priests, Thomas

Three Knights enter and announce their business. They demand to see the Archbishop and brush aside the First Priest's request that they have dinner first. Thomas enters and, despite the threatening demeanour of the Knights, asks that he be left alone with them. In derisive tones the Knights accuse Thomas of ingratitude towards the King, on whose 'urgent business' they purport to come. Thomas rejects their charge that he has betrayed the King and asserts his loyalty, 'saving his order'. The Knights make to attack Thomas, but the Priests interpose themselves. In calmer, but menacing tones, the Knights accuse Thomas of stirring up trouble against the King and rejecting his offers of friendship. Finally, Becket is arraigned for denying the legality of the coronation of the King's son. When Thomas refuses to withdraw the order of excommunication and proclaims his higher loyalty to the law of Christ's Church, he is told that he has spoken in peril of his life. As Thomas leaves, the Knights pursue him with drawn swords. Becket will not leave England; he will stay with his flock.

The entry of the Knights clashes with the mood established in the earlier part of this scene. Order gives way to the harsh 'realities' of 'the world'. The Knights speak with the colloquial vigour of the thug: they talk with urgency of their 'business' – a mere euphemism for 'murder'. Although it is not always easy to distinguish between the Knights as individual characters, the type is instantly recognizable: they cloak their evil under the guise of patriotism. The Priests' offer a dinner is hospitable, but their playing for time is fruitless – the inescapable moment is at hand. The Knights' impatience contrasts with the timeless quality of the earlier part of the play: until this moment, apart from the return of Thomas, very little has happened in terms of plot. Although changes have taken place within the hearts of the characters (Thomas in particular); now we sense the headlong rush of events. Interspersed with the claims that they are acting on behalf of the King are remarks that make it clear the Knights feel personal resentment against Thomas – the tradesman's son who gained the favour of the King. Simple jealousy is clearly one of their motives, and they feel that old scores are about to be settled.

Confronted with this violence and bile, Thomas refuses to be cowed. It is important that he should not go easily to his death, so that any charge that he willed his own martyrdom can be demonstrably refuted. He defends himself, while at the same time being aware that what is about to happen to him is inevitable. The clash of language between persecutors and persecuted is revealing: Thomas is clear, almost legalistic in his defence; the Knights are emotional, repetitive and given to heavy sarcasm. Despite their menace, they are made to seem faintly ridiculous in the face of a power they cannot begin to comprehend. The brute force of the world cannot shake the moral and intellectual power of the Spirit – and, though of course they do not realize it, they are part of the process whereby Thomas achieves sanctity – the Divine scheme even has a place for the Knights; they are a part of Thomas's triumph, which demonstrates the greater glory of God.

In many of their accusations the Knights echo the Tempters. In effect, they accuse Thomas of treasons that he abrogated in the earlier scene. Of course, these treasons were not real treasons. The real treason would be to betray God and His Church and, of course, to do the 'right thing for the wrong reason'. No matter what they threaten, Thomas remains steadfast: to himself, to his Church and to his God.

You are welcome The Priests' politeness contrasts with the Knights' ill-mannered behaviour.

roast your pork A crude pun on what they intend to do to Thomas.

dine upon it Further crudity: they will 'dine out' on the story of their deeds.

The papers in order Thomas is to leave his worldly affairs in order – he is clearly prepared, in all senses, for his death.

the backstairs brat The Knights demonstrate their snobbish jealousy of Thomas, and they are clearly attempting to rile him. Thomas does not rise to their taunts.

the ring Symbol of the office of Archbishop.

Saving my order i.e. Thomas proclaimed his higher loyalty to the Church and to God.

let your order save you A joke is made out of Thomas's proviso.

Now and here The critical moment has arrived.

mention ... dissension The rhyme here emphasizes the feeling that all this has been rehearsed – we are going over old ground.

You had fled from England ... opinions The Knights give their version of recent history. Cf the Second and Third Tempters.

anathema A solemn ecclesiastical curse – part of the rite of excommunication.

evince i.e. defeat.

The King's faithful servants Refers to the bishops whom Becket excommunicated for their part in Prince Henry's coronation.

redounds Reflects.

my people Becket never forgets his responsibility for his flock.

mendicant A beggar.

attaining Depriving of rights by convicting of treason.
It is not Becket i.e. not a personal matter, but one that involves
the question of the supremacy of Church or State.
malfeasance Evil practice (a legal term).
I submit ... of Rome An echo of St Paul, who claimed his
right, as a Roman citizen, to be tried in Rome.

Pages 71–74 The Chorus

The Chorus has smelt the proximity of death and is tormented
by fearful presentiments. The women implicated in the horror
that is about to be performed. They feel shame at their seeming acquiescence, their inability to help Becket.

The speech of the Chorus here overwhelms the reader.
Image after image is juxtaposed to give a picture of hellishness
and disorder, death and corruption. Eliot draws upon the
animal kingdom to convey the beastliness of the act that is
about to be performed. At times, the picture is hinted at rather
than specified – thus 'Scaly wings slanting over' convey the
nameless terror of the nightmare. One is reminded of the
paintings of Hieronymous Bosch. Sometimes the beast is
heard, but not seen – the passage invites the use of all our
senses. Particularly evocative are those images that suggest
corruption in the midst of beauty. Such word-pictures powerfully suggest the essence of martyrdom.

In a mood of terror the Chorus portrays a world in which
the powers of hell have been released upon the earth, as if in
opposition to the martyrdom. It is the protest of evil against
the Will of God – as if this monstrous dance of death is a
demonic resistance to the sanctity that is about to be realized.

Some of the images are self-evidently horrific, but it is not
easy to see why Eliot finds horror and death in the primrose
and the cowslip, for example. All one can say is that in the
world depicted here, evil may underlie even what may seem
beautiful and innocent. The images are not connected and the
effect is to give a picture of chaos as well as horror. The
Chorus seems gripped to the point of hysteria by an instinctive
perception of evil.

The speech is dramatically important. We are about to
witness a murder; a King, who felt his power threatened by a
'turbulent' cleric, has been instrumental in this deed; the
Knights are hired killers, but Eliot wishes us to understand

that more is involved than murder and politics. Thus the universal images of this passage universalize the martyrdom. We are about to witness a moment in history when the hand of God became apparent in the world; inherent in this moment is the triumph of good over the powers of hell. The imagery, which contains a strong hint of the supernatural element in evil, gives the murder a cosmic significance.

subtile Subtle
scaly wings Probably pterodactyls.
heaving of earth Suggests the activity of moles and the activity of the underworld makes itself manifest in our world.
jackass Notable for its unearthly 'laughter'.
jerboa A desert rodent.
loon A bird. Also suggests the maniacal laughter of the lunatic.
ingurgitation Greedy swallowing.
In the guts ... Canterbury Evil is not a thing apart from man – it is inextricably part of him: Original Sin. Thus the Chorus feels implicated in the evil about to be perpetrated.
I have consented The Chorus clearly acknowledges its own guilt. It has been cowardly ('cowered like the wren'); it has been cruel ('Flirted with the passage of the kite')
forgive us An important moment: after confession comes the prayer for forgiveness. The Chorus feels the need to be forgiven not only for its crimes of cowardice and cruelty, but also for the sinful flesh that is part of its nature. The desire to escape the sins of the flesh has led to a fleeting desire to commit suicide as the only way out of its torment.

Pages 74–78 Chorus, Thomas, Priests (The Archbishop's Hall)

Thomas enters and reassures the Chorus: human forgetfulness will cause the memory of present horror to grow dim. The Priests bring news that the Knights are returning: they urge that Thomas should seek refuge in the Cathedral. Thomas refuses to leave, and the Priests eventually have to drag him off by force. To the accompaniment of the *Dies Irae*, the Chorus speaks once again of its fears: this time the emphasis is on Death, the Judgement of God and the prospect of Hell. They conclude with a plea to the Saviour for help in overcoming these fears.

Thomas enters, once again with the word 'Peace'. It is clear that the peace he offers is not yet available to the Chorus, who continue to suffer an agony of hopeless fears. At this stage, they are not able to understand the peace and joy that will come to them when they grasp the insight that God's design has been completed. Clearly, Thomas is not speaking of peace as the world knows it, but he is alluding (as he made plain in the sermon) to the peace that comes to the spirit – and is subsequent upon the death of a martyr. But the Chorus, earth-bound, can see only death, and the horror that may come after death.

Even at this stage in the play, Thomas is able to face the prospect of his own death with equanimity – which represents in itself a triumph over the fears expressed by the Chorus. The difficulty for the actor here, as it is throughout the play, is to present Becket as a man, rather than a mouthpiece for Eliot's ideas on faith, martyrdom and sanctity. In making his will perfect, Becket rather loses touch with common humanity, represented in the play, one supposes, by the Chorus. When Becket refers to himself as not being 'in danger', he is, of course, referring to his immortal soul.

the eternal burden, The perpetual glory The human being must bear the burden of suffering humanity (in this world) but he also has within him the possibility of having a share in the glory of the Kingdom of God. Man is both suffering flesh and eternal spirit.

pierce ... painful joy The words carry on the idea of pain and joy, a part of the human condition.

reality i.e. the reality of the presence of God (in this moment of martyrdom) and the reality of suffering.

shepherd The imagery suggests Christ, 'the Good Shepherd'.

Dies Irae A medieval Latin hymn ('The Day of Wrath'). Here, and at the end of their speech, the Chorus employ a similar rhythm to this hymn:

> Dies irae, dies illa
> Solvet saeclum in favilla.
> Teste David cum Sybilla

Void Hell, involving a sense of emptiness in the soul separated from God. A sense of God's absence. This, according to the Chorus, is more 'horrid than active shapes of hell', which inhabited the Chorus's previous speech and the beginning of this one.

the tree The holy Cross.

my Saviour In extremis, facing the horror of eternal absence from God, the Chorus seeks the intercession of Christ.

Pages 78–82 The Priests, Thomas, The Knights (In the Cathedral)

Thomas insists that the doors of the cathedral remain open. The Priests, desperate to save their master, tell him that the Knights will not respect the sanctuary of the altar – they are maddened beasts, not men. The doors are opened and the Knights enter the cathedral: they are tipsy. Thomas faces his tormentors; he is unafraid. He is murdered.

Thomas's demand that the Priests unbar the door is an obvious testament to his personal courage, but it has a wider significance: the Church may be embattled but it should never become a fortress: it must remain open, even to those who seek its destruction. Ultimately, the Church cannot be violated: its sanctuary remains eternally intact. It endures. The Priests are gently rebuked for 'arguing by results', and one sees what Thomas means. It might be pointed out, however, that Christ enjoins us to know men by their fruit ('The tree is known by his fruit.' Matthew, 12,33), which is surely 'arguing by results'. Thomas suggests that his act will be judged as good or evil according to the standpoint of those who judge it historically. But the martyrdom is properly regarded as being 'out of time'; in other words, it is the design of God, and stands for all eternity. Thus it is not relevant to judge it by worldly standards; this is, of course, a matter of faith. Thomas's martyrdom is not the product of his own will but is the result of the abandonment of his own will to the Will of God.

During this episode, the Knights' drunkenness is admirably captured in the 'jazzy' rhythm of their collective speech, which is strongly reminiscent of Vachel Lindsay's poem 'Daniel Jazz' (1920); it is tempting to believe that Eliot had this poem in mind – he is known to have liked the music! The speeches of Thomas, in contrast, are sturdy and unflinching in tone; self-assertive and hard-edged.

The staging of Becket's murder is probably best done ritualistically – in a stylized manner. This would accord with the liturgical element, which has often been apparent in the play, and would stress the sacrificial element of Becket's death.

Daniel Daniel 6,16–20 Daniel was protected from the lions by the Lord. The Knights here are taunting Thomas; they believe that the Lord will not protect him, but the irony is on them.

mark of the best See Revelation 13,16 and 19,20. The reference
is to the end of the world, when the so-called Beast will enjoy
dominion over the earth. All will receive his 'mark'. The
Knights 'confess' their kinship! Becket destroyed the Beast when
he defeated the Tempters.
Lamb Again the reference is to Revelation. The lamb symbolizes
the force for good, and therefore the opponent of the Beast. The
'Lamb of God' is Christ; His blood washes away man's sins.
absolve Pardon.
temporal vassal Fitz Urse. Thomas was Fitz Urse's feudal lord.
Denys First Bishop of Paris, martyred in 280.

Pages 82–84 The Chorus

As Becket is murdered, the Chorus feel that the whole uni-
verse has been soiled by the act. The horror of the deed far
outstrips anything they have known before – during the times
when they were 'living and partly living'. They feel the need
for a universal cleansing to take place: every part of creation
must be washed. It has all been defiled, including themselves.

The murder of Becket takes place in the world; the sin is
committed by members of the human race and hence the
Chorus's feeling of involvement. The killing is a distillation of
man's inhumanity to man. The insistence that everything
must be cleansed is a reaction to the horror the poor women
witness; it is a positive response, because an awareness of guilt
is a necessary prerequisite of forgiveness.

Clear ... clean ... wash them The repetitions in the verse here
have an obsessional quality, indicative of the guilt the Chorus
feels for the crime that is being committed.
Where is England? The Chorus has lost all sense of place. Later,
the sense of time also disappears. It is as if the event is taking place
outside time and place – it is for all places and for all time.
land of barren boughs An allusion to Dante's *Inferno*. Suicides
appeared in a vision to the poet in the shape of trees with
broken boughs, which bled.
hold season The Chorus, in shock, wants time to stand still.
instant eternity Refers to that moment in time when a person
may have a perception, or glimpse, of eternity. For the Chorus,
this moment is happening now, and is also standing for all time
– having an existence in eternity. Thus, the murder of Becket is
not merely an event in the past – the Chorus unconsciously
perceive that the evil moment will live for ever. It will be
presented one day in a play, in 1935!

Pages 84–90 The Four Knights

After the Knights have murdered Thomas, they address the audience. In 'modern' colloquial prose, they give their version of events, in the hope that the audience will grant them a fair hearing as they endeavour to justify their actions. The First Knight, Reginald Fitz Urse, introduces the other speakers in turn. It is the contention of the Third Knight that he and his accomplices acted from impersonal motives: patriotism and loyalty to the King demanded that they kill Thomas. Even so, he acknowledges that for political reasons the King will probably disown them and thus they cannot hope to derive any personal advancement from their deed – exile will be their probable fate.

The Second Knight argues that Becket was behaving unreasonably when he refused to subordinate his loyalty to the Church to the loyalty that he owed to his King. He accuses Becket of adopting a high-handed attitude in his refusal to combine the offices of Chancellor and Archbishop. Furthermore, if we agree that the Church is now properly subordinated to the State, then we should give him and his friends the credit for taking the initial steps that brought about this situation.

The Fourth Knight concludes that Becket may properly be said to have brought about his own death while a victim of religious mania. He asks that we remember Becket's provocative attitude to them and his refusal to bar the doors against their onslaught. This refusal to escape can only be interpreted as suicidal. The First Knight closes proceedings by urging his listeners to proceed home quietly, making no disturbance.

The introductory remarks of the First Knight immediately arouse your suspicions: we have just witnessed their drunken arrival at the cathedral and the brutal murder of Thomas; therefore it is unlikely that we shall be taken in by his appeal to our patriotism and his request that we maintain an open mind during the speeches that follow. None the less, we should take their arguments seriously because much of what they say is true, and, when occasion demands, they are masters of the half-truth. We can safely dismiss much of what the Third Knight says about his reluctance to kill the Archbishop as mere clap-trap, and his apparent admiration for the manner of Thomas's death is insulting. It is true that the Knights will not benefit from the murder they committed, but the fact that many criminals do not benefit from the proceeds of their crime cannot be regarded as a justification for that crime. Furthermore, his credibility is severely strained, when the Knight claims that they were not personally motivated: the evidence clearly shows that they hated and envied Becket.

The Second Knight is more subtle than the earlier speakers, and his argument goes to the heart of the matter: in his view Thomas was wrong not to find a compromise that could permit the unification of the temporal and spiritual views of life. The subject of much of the play made manifest by the inner debate within Thomas, has made clear that the temporal and the spiritual worlds are essentially opposed. The contemptuous note in this speaker's voice is unmistakable – his is the voice of the politician or the secular historian. The invitation that we should return a verdict of suicide on Thomas's murder (the Fourth Knight) is clever, but carries ingenuity to its limits. The voice here is of the psychologist-cum-historian: it is plausible only if we forget our experience of the play.

We beg you ... attention Ingratiating. The tone of sweet reasonableness contrasts vividly with the behaviour of the Knights which we have just witnessed.

sympathies ... with the under dog The speeches of the Knights abound in clichés – a sign of their insincerity.

Trial by Jury A privilege they had not granted to Thomas.

a man of action ... words Another cliché. The actions of the Knights cannot be justified.

'Hear! Hear!' The Knights are prone to mutual praise.

four plain Englishmen Patriotism: the refuge of the scoundrel.

awfully sorry A grotesque colloquialism – utterly inappropriate in the circumstances.

disinterested Again, not supported by the evidence in the play.

emotional claptrap Aptly describes much of what the Knights say!

Matilda Mother of Henry II.

irruption Invasion.

I read it in your faces Self-deception, surely.

such temperate measures Much of what the Knights say has an unintentionally comic effect.

we who took the first step The audience is here forced to take the Knights' view seriously. It is a fact that many historians might agree with the Third Knight. A disconcerting thought!

Who killed the Archbishop? We are apparently in the realm of detective fiction!

Suicide while of Unsound Mind The view of secular
psychology. For all the plausibility of the Knights (and they *are*
plausible, if absurd), they cannot disguise the sacrilege and
brutality we have witnessed, nor cause us to forget Thomas's
sermon – both of which provide a definitive response to their
attempts at self-justification.

Pages 90–94 The Priests and the Chorus

The doubts of the First Priest are stilled by the certainty of the
Third Priest that the Church has been strengthened by the
persecution of Thomas: Martyrs affirm the supremacy of the
faith. The lost souls are the Knights, condemned to a life of
physical and spiritual desolation. The Second Priest joins the
First Priest in a prayer that Thomas will remember them –
now that he has become united with the other saints and
martyrs in Heaven. The speech of the Chorus, which concludes the play, is in the form of a song of thanksgiving and
praise for the blessing that God has granted to Canterbury.
Finally, they ask God for forgiveness and mercy, while
acknowledging their sinfulness and weakness.

The initial hesitancy of the First Priest gives the opportunity for the Third Priest to strike a contrastingly affirmative
note, which introduces the keynote of the play's coda. Clearly,
we should regard the words as being addressed to the audience and present-day readers of the play, as much as to the
Priests and the Chorus. The revivifying effect of the death of
martyrs upon the Church is unequivocally stated. The spiritually dead Knights are pictured in the vivid imagery as
wandering the earth seeking distraction and forgetfulness to
ward off their sense of inner desolation: it is a powerful evoca-
tion of the soul alienated from God and Nature, inhabiting a
world of hellish extremes and pointless activity.

In contrast the Chorus, inspired by the martyrdom of
Thomas and the new understanding that has come upon
them, are able to reconcile themselves to the world they inhabit. Whereas previously they had spoken of their lives in
terms of endless fear and drudgery, they are now able to
see the hand of God in all things: they are comforted and
strengthened by the restoration of their faith. The brutality
and sin involved in the martyrdom of their beloved Thomas
has been transcended; the design of the Creator has been

perceived in this most degrading of murders. This insight has given them strength to overcome their own terrors and drudgeries: God has not deserted them and they have the inner resources to cope with their lives and the prospect of death. Thomas is asked to pray for them – they have him as an intermediary in heaven between themselves and God.

bereft Deprived of a loved one (by death).
desecrated Violated by profane hands.
Gates of Hercules The Straights of Gibraltar.
libidinous Lustful. The Priest is apparently unaware that Islam is, in fact, a puritanical religion.
And we must ... of you Note the dismissive flatness of this line.
Te Deum A hymn, praising God. The whole speech has a liturgical rhythm.
sightseers ... guide-books The Chorus 'foresees' the fate that awaits the Cathedral in the twentieth century! An anachronism.
Iona The island in the Inner Hebrides, famed for the monastery founded by St Columba (521–597).

Revision questions on Part 2

1 How effective do you find the opening moments of Part 2 of the play? Show what you think Eliot is striving to achieve in the speeches before the entry of the Knights.
2 What initial impressions do the Knights make on their entry into the drama?
3 Comment upon the manner in which Becket deals with the Knights' accusations.
4 How far do you find what the Knights say is related to the temptations Becket underwent in Part 1?
5 Should Becket have made more effort to save his own life?
6 What part is played by the Priests in the Second Part?
7 Compare and contrast the emotional impact of the successive major speeches of the Chorus in Part 2 of the play.
8 How would you stage the murder of Becket?
9 Summarize the Knights' arguments. Do you find their arguments convincing?
10 Describe the mood of the end of the play in the light of the final utterance of the Chorus.

The characters

Becket

The last temptation is the greatest treason:
To do the right deed for the wrong reason.

The action of the play deals only with the ending of Becket's life; thus we are not given an opportunity to watch him develop over an extended period – as we are, say, with Macbeth or any other of Shakespeare's tragic heroes. Nevertheless, Eliot contrives to present us with a full, rounded portrait of Becket; he dominates the play, even when he is not on-stage. His presence is initially perceived through the thoughts and feelings of the Chorus and the Priests. To the Chorus he represents a threat: his return is seen as a disruption in their humdrum lives; they would rather be left alone. To the Priests he is the leader of whom they have been deprived for seven years – they look for his return to provide some stability in their lives; and for him to defend the Church against secular encroachment. Thus, early in the play, Eliot establishes the centrality of Becket before we meet him. As yet, however, he is essentially an abstraction: expectations are high, but what sort of man is it who must bear the burden of people's hopes and be the focus of their fears?

Becket's entry into the drama immediately establishes him as a defender of the weak: he rebukes the Priests for their arrogant disparagement of the Chorus, hinting that the women's understanding of events may be deeper than they themselves realize. Also, in his somewhat riddling opening speech, Becket raises the spiritual and intellectual level of the play; and the audience is invited to consider the paradoxical nature of faith, action and the Will of God.

Becket's past is laid before the audience during the episode with the Tempters. Here we learn, for example, something of the gaiety and sensuality of his youth, and of his proficiency as Chancellor. More significantly, the conflict that arose (between Church and State; the spiritual and the secular) when Becket was made Archbishop, is outlined by the Second Tempter. We perceive, too, on a personal level, the conflict Becket felt between love for the King and the demands of office: harmony persisted during the time of Becket's Chancel-lorship, but discord came with his accession to the Archbishopric.

Skilfully, and in dramatic form, Eliot thus presents us with Becket's history – we learn of what has led up to this state of affairs. Becket emerges as a man who, while conscious of the good things in life and aware of the fruits of office, is unwilling to compromise on matters of principle. On a still more per-sonal level, the unruffled way in which he deals with the temptation to turn the clock back, renew his friendship with the King and ignore what he feels to be his destiny, reveals a confidence in himself that is born out of the certainty of his faith. It is fitting that his anger should be aroused by the Third Tempter, who seeks to inveigle him into a faction against the King; he refuses to be a figurehead of rapacious barons, and dismisses the temptation with the utmost contempt.

Throughout the first three temptations, Becket has demon-strated complete control of himself and of his assailants. With the arrival of the Fourth Tempter, we feel that Becket be-comes more 'engaged' than he has hitherto been. The battles with the first Tempters were all in the past; they could not touch him. The Fourth Tempter, in offering him the tempta-tion of martyrdom, but motivated by the deadly reason of spiritual pride, touches a nerve that gives the scene particular drama and pertinency. Becket's struggle becomes much more pronounced: it is clear that he is wrestling with the Tempter (and thus, of course, with himself) in 'reality', whereas the previous temptations were merely shadows. For a start, the temptation comes as a surprise, and its potency is obvious when Thomas reveals that he has already thought of the temptation to seek martyrdom – with its attendant eternal glory. Thus Thomas is faced with the prospect of damnation, even though to stand firm in the face of death is the right thing to do. Thomas faces despair as he listens to the Tempter speak back at him his opening words – a means by which Eliot emphasizes that, despite the objective presence of the Tempter on stage, Thomas is essentially carrying out an inner debate.

Thomas faces his motivation for action and momentarily withdraws from the scene. When we next meet him, he pro-nounces himself reconciled to whatever may be about to hap-pen to him. The precise means by which his way becomes clear is not shown to us – Eliot presents it rather as a 'mystery', in the religious sense. We are asked to take on trust that Becket's certainty and resolution emerge from the temptations and that his decision is an act of faith in God, into whose hands he commits himself absolutely. Becket's character may none the less be said to have developed. His sermon reveals in more detail the source of his new-found inner security; the prose is poised and precisely-argued: martyrdom springs from the will of God and not from the will of the martyr. It is an act of submission, in which the martyr abandons self, that the will of God may go forward. Throughout the speech Becket speaks to us in tones of loving humility – the very antithesis of spiritual pride – yet it is a voice that rings with the self-confidence of deep faith.

It remains for Becket to face his persecutors. He parries their threats and insults with calm courage; he dismisses their jibes with a note of irony and satirizes their pretensions to loyalty to the King. He does not go meekly to the slaughter but submits his cause to 'the judgement of Rome'. As the moment of his death approaches, he courageously refuses to allow the door of God's cathedral to be barred against his murderers: he is the still, calm centre in the midst of rant, chaos and outrage. In his final speeches he demands that the Knights do not touch his flock and dies with words of Christ-like surrender to Almighty God.

Although the end is inevitable, Eliot gives Becket sufficient dramatic interest during Part 2 to sustain our involvement in what happens to him: as he battles with the Knights he emerges clearly as a human being (just as he did when he battled with the Tempters), and the charge that he is a mere abstraction, epitomizing saintliness, cannot be sustained.

The Chorus

And meanwhile we have gone on living,
Living and partly living . . .

In common with their Greek antecedents, the Chorus (consisting of the poor women of Canterbury) is employed to establish a mood at the outset of the play. They express a sense of foreboding, and feel they are forced to witness some terrible act from which they would prefer to avert their gaze.

Subject to occasional oppression and the demands of labour, they lead essentially meaningless lives. the established routines, the seasonal rote, while bringing few pleasures, at least have the merit of providing a sort of security – but the Chorus are apathetic and alienated Yet they fear change. They are devoid of a spiritual dimension in their lives. Inevitably, they remind us of twentieth-century man: they provide us with an immediate point of contact within the play; Eliot probably intends that we should identify with them. Thus, having formed this early bond with the Chorus, we too become witnesses to the martyrdom; we share their doubts, fears and moral cowardice. By the end of the play, perhaps we can share their renewal of faith and purpose.

To the poor women, the return of Thomas is a threat; they are sure it will bring disaster upon them; they feel unequal to the strain of being caught up in events over which they can have no control. Naturally enough, the safer course would be for Thomas to leave them. Of course, they are right in one sense: things can never be the same once they have witnessed the martyrdom. True to the theme of the play, they come, like Thomas, to find themselves both passive witnesses of the action and involved in it – like the martyr, they are both agents and patients.

As the play unfolds we find the mood of the Chorus becoming closely identified with that of Becket. Thus, after the Temptation, their despair is a reflection of Thomas's own feeling of God's desertion. Similarly, after his sermon we find the Chorus echoing the sentiments they had heard expressed that Christmas morning. They have not lost their sense of dread and their waiting is still agonizing, but their perceptions have developed and they are able to look beyond the immediacy of suffering towards the possibility of renewal. This is a considerable advance upon their early state of mind.

Intuitively, the Chorus is acutely aware of the evil in the world, which is made manifest by the Knights. Their understanding, while not complete, none the less grasps that, in common with all humanity, they live in a fallen world, where the powers of darkness co-exist with the powers of light. Good and evil are inextricably mixed; indeed evil may inhabit that which is apparently good and attractive. They are also able to perceive the triumph of Thomas over the wickedness that threatened to overwhelm him. The martyr's death offers hope that wickedness shall not be victorious. The strength of the faith is proclaimed by the martyr's preparedness to die for it, and the manner of his death takes away the terror of death itself. Thus, the Chorus finds that their faith has been reawakened by the events they have witnessed. A further development is made manifest in the final speech, when they are able to call upon the prayers of Thomas; no longer do they wish him away, for he has become their intermediary in Heaven.

The process of the Chorus's re-establishment of faith has not been easy: they have had to come to terms not only with the evil in the world but also with the evil in themselves – at one point in the play they acknowledge their own implication in what happened to Thomas. The collective personality of the Chorus has progressed from apathy and fear, through despair and guilt, to enlightenment and faith in God's Will. It has not been a smooth progress – there have been backslidings and uncertainties – but the final note of harmony is clear.

The Priests

Even now, in sordid particulars
The eternal design may appear.

Despite their education, the understanding of the Priests is arguably inferior to that of the Chorus. Like the poor women, whom they tend to patronize, they look anxiously for the return of Thomas. They have a more sophisticated appreciation of the political situation and seem at times more concerned for the welfare of the Church (and indirectly themselves) than with the spiritual welfare of their flock. Thus, seeking peace, they enquire about the possibility of a reconciliation between the King and the Archbishop. Eliot presents the Priests as ecclesiastical civil servants: they appreciate the delicacy of the situation and perceive the dangers inherent in the pride of Becket, now that it is in conflict with the pride of the King. They sense too that a change is coming upon them – but they tend to be fatalistic, seeing flux as the state of things. It is significant that the Priests strongly urge that Thomas should preserve his life in the face of the Knights' assault – they are worldly men.

As characters, the Priests are not strongly individualized. The *Second Priest*, perhaps, seems unduly obsessed with trivial details, such as the laying of a fire in Thomas's room, and he is snobbish and dismissive of the Chorus. The under-standing of the *First Priest* seems even less than that of his brethren: he totally fails to grasp the significance of the mar-tyrdom and has to have it explained to him by the Third Priest, who is clearly the most spiritual and intellectually gifted of the trio. At the end of the play, they are granted insight into the true significance of Thomas's martyrdom, but even the speech of the *Third Priest* seems pale beside the glory of the Chorus's final utterance.

The Tempters

All things are unreal,
Unreal or disappointing . . .

The Tempters are the means chosen by Eliot to present dra-matically the struggle within the mind and heart of Thomas – all seek to divert him from his chosen course.

The *First Tempter* offers a return to the past: to abandon the hardship of spiritual struggle and embrace a life of sensual ease. The appeal is powerfully laced with nostalgia, as Thomas is reminded of his early days, when as a young man he led a life of pleasure. All that Thomas needs to do to re-capture such moments is to patch up his quarrel with the King. The temptation is given added force by the jocular intimacy of the First Tempter and the undoubted sensual beauty and music of the poetry. Individualizing the character is as much a matter of style as it is of content. The fluidity of the verse alters abruptly as this Tempter becomes aware that he is not having any success: the phrases are clipped and the sweetness becomes heavy sarcasm.

The *Second Tempter* suggests that Thomas should subordin-ate the spiritual life to temporal matters. As a political bishop Thomas could do much to alleviate the condition of the poor and by such means attain to earthly glory. He could make a name for himself by the proper administration of justice and the institution of some much needed reforms. Again, Eliot captures exactly the right voice in the verse, as the Second Tempter adopts the fruity tones of the accomplished politi-cian, who is well able to deal with weighty abstractions. His temptation, however, comes to grief: Thomas is simply not interested in temporal power that has no spiritual foundation.

There is some subtlety in the *Third Tempter*, who takes a

positive delight in his plain speaking. Thomas has little difficulty in resisting the temptation to sell himself and his
authority to the power-seeking baronial classes. The brusque-
ness of manner evident in the Third Tempter matches the
crudity of his appeal: Thomas is not interested in pursuing
self-aggrandisement by leading a rebellion against the King,
nor is he taken in by the specious appeal to 'liberty' etc.

The *Fourth Tempter*, in suggesting that Thomas should
pursue martyrdom, poses an unexpected and serious threat.
This Tempter's tone and manner of speech are remarkably
similar to those of Thomas himself, and by this means, Eliot
presents us in dramatic form with the innermost secrets of
Thomas's heart: we find revealed the lure of spiritual pride. In
pursuing martyrdom for reasons of self-glorification, Thomas
would be putting himself in the place of God and risking
external damnation.

Thus the debate between Thomas and Tempter presents us
with the dramatic and thematic core of the play. If Thomas
cannot act for the right reasons, then what he does must
inevitably be sinful. Eliot suggests the close correspondence
between Tempter and tempted by having the Fourth Tempter
both quote and echo Thomas's own words and nuances of
speech. In one sense, of course, Thomas is talking to himself.
The confusion of motives, which must be resolved, is vividly
set before us in this episode.

The Knights

We have served your interests; we merit your
applause; and if there is any guilt whatever
in the matter, you must share it with us.

Initially, the Knights are presented as a collective personality:
their manner is abrupt and hostile; they accuse Thomas of
disloyalty to the King and demand that he absolve the excommunicated bishops. When Thomas refuses to comply, their
manner becomes even more threatening. They murder
Thomas in a drunken rage.

After the murder, as expressions of various attitudes, they
become more individualized, but despite their more 'civilized'
tone they remain embodiments of men reduced to the level of
beasts – devoid of any appreciation of the spiritual significance of the act of which they have been part. At the end of

the play they are pictured as lost souls, wandering the earth without resting place or shelter in the hell of their alienation from God.

The Knights' prose address to the audience reveals something of their personalities. The *First Knight* behaves as a sort of master of ceremonies, introducing the others, while making a specious plea for fair play when we come to judge them. The *Third Knight* does not advance any positive reasons for killing Becket; like the First Knight, he relies on cliché and half-truth to deceive the audience – he is transparently ridiculous in his attempt to claim that he is disinterested. We are not moved to agree with him, for we have just witnessed the scenes in which the Knights confronted Becket and were clearly shown to be motivated, to a considerable degree, by spite and personal antipathy.

The Second and Fourth Knights, with greater respect for our intelligence, seek to alter our perception of the murder. Both adopt a manner of apparent reasonableness and put forward subtle arguments. The *Second Knight* contends that Thomas was wrong in not permitting the temporal and spiritual worlds to be combined in his person. Cleverly, he bases his appeal on the belief with which many of his hearers would agree, that it is proper for the functions of Church and State to be separate. He is confident that he will find in the audience few lovers of a theocracy. It is all very plausible, until we remember that they had demanded that Becket should combine the temporal and the spiritual – by surrendering to the King's wishes. The *Fourth Knight* expresses the view that Becket, in not seeking to avoid death, has, in effect, committed suicide. The degree to which we find this monstrous and ridiculous will depend upon how far we have been influenced in our perception of Becket during the play. It may be disconcerting to reflect that this Knight's view would coincide with the interpretation of the secular historian and psychologist.

It will be clear, from a cursory study of the Knights, that their viewpoints after the event to some extent mirror the views of the Tempters before the murder. Dramatically, they force the audience to assess their own reaction to the events they have just witnessed; this is facilitated by the easy-mannered, 'modern' prose that characterizes their speeches. They nevertheless remain, in essence, an embodiment of men without God, living in a state of brutish materialism.

Structure and style

Themes of the play

Martyrdom: 'Living and partly living'

At the outset of the play the Chorus, who for thematic purposes may be taken to represent common humanity (in all places and for all times), stands in dread of some cataclysmic event. Their lives, rooted in the pains and small pleasures of physical existence, are dimly perceived to be about to be disrupted by an event which goes beyond the customary experience of 'living and partly living'. Specifically, they appear to be in awe of the supernatural, which seems about to invade their temporal world: 'Destiny waits in the hand of God, shaping the still unshapen ...'. It is, perhaps, an awareness of a spiritual dimension beyond worldliness that draws them mysteriously to the Cathedral to await what is to happen. It would seem partly to be inspired by a need for protection. Yet they sense the danger, even though at this stage they perceive their role to be no more than that of passive witnesses. Thus is portrayed the plight of humanity: listless and lost – seeking meaning beyond the physical facts of life, yet pusillanimous before the awesomeness of the supernatural.

The way to salvation

As the drama unfolds, the Chorus is forced to witness the events surrounding Thomas's return and murder; their gradual but ever-increasing involvement in the destiny of their Archbishop leads them, through travail, to a new understanding of themselves, the world and their place in God's creation: in a sense, they are reborn. In Part 1 of the play, the poor women focus their need for protection on Thomas himself, but it is clear from his sermon that he does not offer them peace 'as the world knows it'. It is not so much protection that they need, as salvation – and it is as a means to their salvation (and ours) that Thomas offers his life to God. In this way, the martyrdom is a re-enactment of Our Lord's Sacrifice upon the Cross.

Reconciliation

Before salvation, in religious terms, is possible, the Chorus has to pass first from a mere passive acceptance of the evil in the world to a painful understanding of their own participation in this sin. The realization of guilt is vividly captured just prior to the murder episode: 'I have consented, Lord Archbishop, have consented' and again, just after the murder: 'We are soiled by a filth we cannot clean . . .'. In theological terms, the Chorus is expressing the burden of guilt for the sin that it must bear for being members of the fallen human race, and this links it with the act which the Knights have just perpetrated before our eyes.

Alongside the acceptance of guilt goes the expression of a need for cleansing: 'Clean the air! . . . take the stone from the stone . . . the skin from the arm . . . wash the brain, wash the soul, wash them, wash them!' This urgent appeal to be cleansed does not go unanswered in the play. God responds, through His Son, by means of his saints and martyrs – Thomas in particular – to the prayers of His fallen creatures. The repentance of the Chorus for their apathy and complicity in sin proves a fruitful soil for the Holy Spirit to nurture the human soul. In the final speech of the play, the Chorus, on behalf of all, offers a prayer for forgiveness and mercy – and is able to invite the intercession of Thomas: 'Blessed Thomas, pray for us'.

Thus we are invited to participate during the play, in a religious as well as a dramatic experience. Watching Eliot's unfolding of the martyrdom of Becket may, in some important respects, be regarded as akin to an act of worship. This, of course, hinges upon our capacity to identify ourselves with the Chorus and thus to participate in the redemptive process. The notion of a coincidence between theatre and worship has antecedents in Greek drama.

Commitment to the Will of God

The immediate agent of change within the play is, of course, Thomas himself. He shares with the Chorus the need to accept evil within himself and the world – and to transcend it by commitment of self to the Divine scheme for His creatures. The danger to Thomas's soul is exemplified in his dialogue with the Tempters – in particular, the Fourth Tempter. Martyrdom is open to question here. The martyr, tainted by the sins common to all humanity, may be seeking his own death for reasons of selfish glory – both temporal and spiritual. Is the martyr elevating himself to godhead? Is martyrdom an attempt to buy a passage to Heaven? In short, is it a manifestation of *hubris* – spiritual pride?

These, to some extent, are questions relevant to all who aspire to be Christians, and they apply pre-eminently to martyrs: wrestling with these questions forces Thomas to the point of despair – is there no way that he can shed the taint of mortality? The moment when Thomas, in spiritual crisis, comes to 'make perfect (His) will' is hidden from us: it cannot be dramatized, it is a 'Mystery' of the workings of the Holy Spirit. To some critics, that we do not 'see' Thomas's moment of recognition – the denouement – is a weakness in the play. The sermon on Christmas morning clearly demonstrates, however, the effects of the recognition of the workings of the Holy Spirit within him: Thomas has achieved the abandonment of self, in faith, to the Will of God. The murder itself can now stand as a testament to the transcending of death and sin. Thomas sacrifices himself for his belief and as a witness to the faith that inspires him. In so doing, he inspires the Chorus to a rebirth of faith in the design of God.

Martyrdom: 'witnessing'

In the original Greek form, the word 'martyr' means simply 'witness'; it came later to be specifically associated with the idea of *dying* for a belief. In *Murder in the Cathedral* we see both senses of the word demonstrated. The witnessing of the Chorus involves both being active and passive at the same time (both agent and patient). The play deals with the paradox that a person may be both an 'actor' (doer) and acted upon at the same moment, like the audience of a play, who both passively watch and influence the performance on stage. At times the poor women reflect a prevailing mood, but it is evident, too, that their 'witness' in the original sense of the word is a necessary ingredient in the make up of Thomas's martyrdom; using the word here in its later sense ('witnessing unto death').

Thomas's death as a martyr cannot, as we have seen, be

regarded as personal or selfish to Thomas himself; on the contrary, the martyr's death is a means whereby God restores the faith of the spiritually moribund and reconciles mankind to Himself. If Thomas's act is to have any meaning, it must have witnesses – it is this function that the Chorus fulfils, and while they do so they move out of their initial role as watchers and waiters and become actively engaged in the process that is taking place. The act of not averting their collective gaze entails them in moral activity; so does the recognition of their guilt and their subsequent confession. At the end, it is their prayer for forgiveness and plea for Thomas's intercession that make possible their redemption. The paradox is resolved in the way in which the Chorus are therefore both active and passive: to be complete the martyrdom demands that they are both agents and patients.

In the same way, Thomas is called upon both to act and to suffer. At one point in the play, the apparent conflict seems insuperable: if Thomas actively pursues martyrdom then he becomes a victim of spiritual pride; equally to do nothing, and simply wait or evade the issue would be an act of moral cowardice. It is only by an act of faith and committal of self to God that the martyrdom becomes 'purified'. In his own self, Thomas is called upon to reconcile being both agent and patient – once again this entails an act of faith, in which the self is subsumed in the Divine purpose.

The temporal and the spiritual

A significant theme in the play is the conflict between temporal and spiritual values. Thomas as a friend of the King, who became Chancellor – and later Archbishop – serves as an embodiment of this clash of values. His refusal to accede to the King's wish to reinstate the excommunicated bishops, indeed his excommunication of them in the first instance, represents a refusal to compromise his beliefs and his Church in the interests of temporal expediency. To restore the bishops would seem to be the sensible thing to do, but to do so would be a betrayal of self, Church and, ultimately, God. It is likely that Eliot, writing in a secular age, was acutely aware of the spiritual compromises, both individual and ecclesiastical, of his time. The play exemplifies what such compromises mean.

It is Thomas's perception that the Church must be in the

world, but not of the world. The worldly Church, which subordinates its spiritual function as Christ's Mystical Body on earth to the demands of materialism, is Godless and barren. The Priests, in their concern over details of physical wellbeing, and their understandable but misguided desire that Thomas should preserve his life, are not Godless men; but they are limited in so far as they fail to see that the Church can only be meaningfully preserved if Thomas lives out the Will of God – even at the expense of his life. As the Priests eventually come to realize, it is from the death of Thomas that new life can come to the Church: that the deaths of her saints and martyrs, acting in the spirit of Christ, are a means to the nourishment of the souls that comprise His Body, His Church.

Structure

The story relates the final days of Becket: the basic situation is conveyed by the Chorus and the Priests; Becket returns to Canterbury; he is tempted and overcomes temptation; he preaches a sermon; the Knights arrive and kill him; the Knights present their 'justification'; there is an epilogue spoken by Priests and Chorus. It will be clear from this bald summary that there are very few 'events' in the sense of physical happenings on stage. No sub-plots complicate the action, and the historical background, where necessary, is sketched in obliquely by reference. Even the most blatant physical act, the actual murder, is presented in a ritualized manner – and thus distanced from the audience – rather than as an act of slaughter. Eliot's purpose would seem to be to direct our attention inwards, to what is happening within the characters and towards our consideration of the theological issues in the play.

The division of the play into two parts, with Becket's sermon forming a middle portion, neatly reflects the structure of the play. Part 1 centres dramatic interest on the conflict within Thomas: we see him tempted to return to the past and to become a martyr for the wrong reasons. Tension increases with the power exerted over him by the Fourth Tempter. The crisis comes and is resolved. There is a pause while Thomas preaches his sermon, which presents the audience with an understanding of martyrdom. Then Part 2 unfolds the consequences of the decision made at the end of Part 1. Inevitably, there may be some slackening of dramatic tension here, precisely because the consequence is inevitable (and already known to the audience, because Becket is an historical character).

Part 2 maintains our interest because it not only has more overt action, but also because we can observe the effects of the murder upon the Chorus, with whom we have always felt ourselves identified. We may also note in this context the sudden emergence of the Knights into 'our present' – a remarkable theatrical coup.

In structure, *Murder in the Cathedral* resembles Greek tragic drama. Here we find the Chorus and the story focusing upon the last hours of the protagonist; also, we find that the play deals with a single situation in which man is seen wrestling with the Divine Will, which is shaping the way things happen. Of course, Eliot is writing Christian drama and thus the play, though it portrays the death of the hero, is seen in the catastrophe to be triumphant, not tragic. The Chorus, too, unlike its Greek counterpart, is involved in the action as distinct from standing to one side as an observer and mediator between action and audience. Furthermore, Greek tragedy traditionally concerned itself with the passing of twenty-four hours, whereas Eliot's play depicts the passing of about twenty-seven days.

The theme of spiritual rebirth has also a shaping influence upon the play: the pattern of sin (alienation from God – confession . . . repentance – sacrifice – renewal) is familiar to Christians and is given expression in Christian liturgy, particularly in the Eucharist. We are given explicit reminders of this pattern in the poetry of the play, which frequently quotes, or echoes, the service of Holy Communion.

Literary terms

Action (in drama) Usually refers to physical action on stage, by means of which a story is told. But it is not necessarily external or physical – it may involve the revelation of a character's inner thoughts and feelings, as they develop or change during the play. It may mean simply 'plot'.

Anachronism An occurrence that takes place in an inappropriate time setting; e.g. The Knights' address to the audience is 'anachronistic'.

Alliteration Occurs when words beginning with the same sound are placed in close proximity.

Blank verse Unrhymed verse, in ten-syllable lines.

Chronicle play Historical events enacted in a stage play.

Cliché A hackneyed, over-used phrase.

Climax A crucial moment of high emotional intensity. Usually occurs just before the resolution of the drama, or at some significant phase in the drama.

Colloquial Words that are used in everyday speech.

Drama Means 'action' or 'that which is performed'. Refers to stage plays of all types.

Dramatic irony Occurs when a character in a play speaks words the full significance of which he does not recognize. The audience, assumed to be in full possession of the facts, does appreciate the full significance of what is said.

Imagery Any figurative use of language. Often 'word pictures' that utilize the capacity of the mind to respond emotionally to an idea evoked by the words.

Irony Occurs when the real meaning of what is expressed is at variance with what appears to be said, i.e. the surface meaning is in conflict with what is really meant.

Liturgical drama Plays that are related to the forms adopted by the Church in acts of public worship, especially the Mass or Eucharist.

Metaphor A comparison that is unequivocally implied or expressed (without the use of 'like ...' or 'as').

Morality play A type of 'liturgical drama'. Similarly, 'Miracle play'.

Paradox An apparent contradiction or absurdity, which, on closer examination, is revealed to contain an essential truth.

Personification An abstract idea treated as though it were a person.

Plot Narrative or events placed in a time-sequence, which makes up a story.

Rhythm Language has a natural distribution of sound-emphasis, sometimes called 'stress' or 'rhythm'. When the stresses occur regularly, it is called 'metre'. Poets often arrange the stresses in lines to enhance the understanding of what they write, or to cause us to read the line in a prescribed manner.

Simile A figure of speech, introduced by 'like' or 'as', which compares two essentially different things.

Tragedy At its simplest, a tragedy describes the 'fall' of a character. It usually describes the sufferings of this character, whose fate may be predetermined by the gods – it ends in the death of the 'tragic hero'.

Style

Verse

In the planning stage, *Murder in the Cathedral* was to be in prose. It was at the suggestion of a friend and mentor, Rupert Doone, that the Choric passages were rendered in verse, and later the whole play became the verse-drama with which we are now familiar. It was the first of a number of successful and well-regarded verse-dramas that Eliot was to write.

Eliot consciously wrote in a form of flexible verse that is different from the Shakespearean iambic blank verse; he was aware of the futility and dangers in seeking to emulate the inimitable. Some experience with the handling of verse as a dramatic medium was gained from *The Rock* – a pageant play performed by amateurs at Sadler's Wells in 1934.

Eliot's versification owes much to the medieval play *Everyman* (and other plays of the Miracle/Morality tradition) – particularly in his use of alliteration and occasional rhyme. The variation in line-length is similarly derived, but much more pronounced in *Murder in the Cathedral*. The chief glories, perhaps, of the play's verse are to be found in the Choric passages. Writing verse which is to be spoken in unison obviously presents special problems: if, for example, a regular metrical pattern is employed there is a danger of monotony, with the consequence that the audience is sent to sleep. Thus we find great variety of metre in the speeches of the Chorus: some lines stretch out to great length, while others are relatively short. Some passages are deliberately regular; some are rhymed. Eliot adapts the precise form of utterance to the needs of the sense he expresses. The monotony of the existence of the poor women is captured in the regularity of rhythm, as they describe themselves as 'living and partly living' (page 19). In the same speech we find the memorable internal rhyme of 'the strain on the brain' of the humble people, and the speech concludes with urgent repetitions and alliterations, which convey the insistence of the Chorus that Thomas should 'leave them'. These long lines contain obvious pauses, which would enable the speaker to take a breath. Furthermore, these breaks would enable the producer of the play to have the speakers move in and out of unison as required – thus contributing to the variety necessary to keep the attention of the audience. Frequently, we see that the Choric speeches end on an incantatory note: repetitious phrases interspersed with emphatic pauses are of the nature of a chant.

It is worth remembering that Eliot adjusts the rhythms of the speeches according to the characters and situations of the speakers: the fussy, mundane concerns of the Priests are often couched in the colloquial rhythms of everyday speech – we are scarcely aware that they are in verse. The clipped utterances of the Knights at times convey the forceful brutality of their natures and mission. The Tempters are clearly differentiated by rhythm. The regularity and fluency, together with the repetitious element in Thomas's first speech, have an immediately reassuring effect upon the listener.

Thus the structure of the verse is precisely used by Eliot to influence the response of the audience and to aid the performer in the play. All is carefully modulated and controlled.

Prose

Prose occurs twice in the play: Becket's Christmas Morning Sermon is in prose; and the Knights address the audience in prose after the murder. In both cases, the effect is startling and Eliot is clearly using prose to capture the attention of the audience at crucial moments in the drama. Both episodes attempt to 'explain' Becket's martyrdom and death: the sermon before, the Knights after, the event. There are important differences between the two passages in style and purpose.

It will immediately strike the reader that the Sermon is couched in prose that is more rhetorical and elevated than everyday speech. It is clearly designed to induce reflection and contemplation in the listeners: we are exhorted to 'consider' and 'reflect'. The passage as a whole is carefully organized: proceeding from text to statement of theme; development of argument; finally to conclusion and reference to the future. In fact, a perfect sermon, illustrated by Biblical reference and quotation and, to some extent, echoing in the long sentences the rhythms of Biblical language. The total effect is to provide a central pause in the play, which puts into perspective the temptations and Becket's decision in Part 1, and what, as a result of this decision, is to occur in Part 2. Thus it is ensured that the audience understands what has happened and is about to happen. It is a moment of calm, distanced in style from the surrounding verse and from the present day, during which matters of the spirit are explicitly expounded. It may be added that it would obviously be inappropriate for a sermon to be in verse.

The style of the Knights' prose is entirely different. They speak the colloquial English of the twentieth century. The incongruity between what is discussed and the manner of presentation gives rise to some ironic comedy, but Eliot expressed the view that he did not wish the comic aspect to be overplayed. The words are cliché-ridden and make specious pleas for 'fair play'. They seek to establish sympathy between speakers and audience; the familiar rhythms ensure that the audience feels 'at home'. The fact that the Knights speak 'our language' to justify their actions emphasizes the distance between twentieth-century modernism and the eternal values exemplified by the play. The effect is precisely the opposite to what the Knights intend: in seeking to make their justification approachable, and in their jocularity of manner, they make their actions less appealing. The gulf between what they have done and our understanding of it has widened throughout the play, and the style of their justifications makes their actions even more unpalatable, not less. Simply, they are made to seem ridiculous. This should not, however, lead us to dismiss their cleverness; they are plausible and their debate-like style forces us to think before we can dismiss what they say.

Imagery

The imagery of the play contributes mightily to its impact upon the audience. Eliot employs his images to give the story life and colour, and to enhance the mood of particular situations. The play is restricted in locale (the so-called 'unity of place' is more or less adhered to), but the sense of a background of everyday circumstances is implied in much of what the Chorus says – particularly in their early speeches. In other words, the imagery paints a backcloth in the imagination, against which the characters live. The imagery of the Chorus frequently derives from the seasonal treadmill to which their lives are found at the beginning of the play. Later, we see how increasingly their images take on a new dimension, as their awareness of a world outside and beyond daily drudgery increases. In a particularly vivid passage, they evoke the presence of evil in the world: 'Corruptions in the dish ...'

(page 73). Thomas's more rarefied, abstract imagery reflects his more subtle, philosophical mind: 'the wheel may turn and still/Be forever still.' The image of the wheel is reiterated during the play and presents one of the central paradoxes of the drama: that one may be agent and patient at one and the same time; or, to put it another way, that Becket is seen to be acting out the Will of God by allowing the Will of God to be acted out upon him. In production, the idea is reinforced theatrically at the moment of the murder, when the Knights ritualistically kill Becket with their swords pointing inwards towards him – in the manner of the spokes of a wheel, with Becket at the hub. It is revealing to study in detail how the Tempters are given their own characteristic imagery, which reflects their particular temptation; their influence can be measured upon Becket by the degree to which it is echoed in his speech.

The Greek element

The most obvious 'borrowing' from Greek drama is the Chorus, used in the play as a mediator between the action on stage and the audience, and also to intensify 'the action by projecting its emotional consequences, so that we the audience see it doubly, by seeing its effect on other people' (Eliot). Eliot further develops the role of the Chorus by having it as a participant in the action. In making most of that action occur off-stage, confining it to virtually a single locale and restricting the time depicted on stage (in comparison with conventional historical drama), Eliot also gives the play a Greek flavour. Greek tragedy was religious drama, owing its origins to ancient pagan rituals, which were designed to banish the darkness and induce the return of Spring; *Murder in the Cathedral* is self-evidently a religious drama, and the ancient folk-pattern is evident in a Christian context. More could be said, but it is worth noting that the play in its concentration on a single situation involving the death of a great man whose destiny is shaped by Divine power, gives further evidence of Greek influence.

The element of ritual

The sense that we are witnessing a religious ritual is significantly present in the play. Arguably, the actual murder of

Thomas demands ritualistic rather than realistic presentation. The scene in which the Priests denote the passage of time, with banners and Introits, obviously calls for ritualized performance. The singing of the *Dies Irae* and later the *Te Deum*, also reminds us of the Christian liturgy.

General questions and sample answer in note form

1 'Becket is insufficiently characterized to make him dramatically interesting.' Discuss.

2 'For all its lack of action and its unconvincing protagonist, *Murder in the Cathedral* is intensely moving and at times exciting when performed.' Discuss.

3 'There is no true action . . . the centre of the play is a state of mind.' Comment on this assertion.

4 Outline how you think *Murder in the Cathedral* should be staged. Give reasons, based upon your understanding of the play's themes, for your opinions.

5 Discuss the importance of the Sermon to the play as a whole.

6 'The moral action of the play, the purification of Becket's will, is insufficiently analysed.' Examine the implications of this remark. How far do you agree with it?

7 Some critics complain that Part 2 of the play fails to sustain our interest, and is dramatically tame when compared with Part 1. Argue a case for or against this proposition.

8 How far do you feel involved with what happens in the play?

9 What is the impact and significance of the Chorus?

10 Do you think *Murder in the Cathedral* has any relevance for a twentieth-century audience?

11 'The theme of the play is martyrdom.' Discuss.

12 Eliot believed that verse in a play must 'justify itself dramatically'. In what ways do you think that the verse in *Murder in the Cathedral* is justified?

13 'We pass with them through horror, out of boredom, into glory.' Discuss with reference to the Chorus.

14 For what purpose and to what effect do you think Eliot employs prose in the play?

15 How effectively do you think the struggle within the heart of Becket is dramatized?

16 'Becket towers above ordinary men but, in the drama of his death, he is a passive and ambiguous figure.' Discuss.

17 How far do you agree that the most powerful writing in

the play is to be found in those passages which deal with the presentation of guilt, uncleanness and the 'void'?

18 Discuss the theme of the conflict between temporal and eternal values, as exemplified in the play.

19 'Can I neither act nor suffer without perdition?' Discuss Thomas's dilemma at this point in the play.

20 'The murder in the cathedral is not primarily a murder at all, but an act of redemption.' What do you think is meant by this remark, and how far do you agree?

Suggested notes for essay answer to question 1

(a) *Introduction*: Eliot dramatizing martyrdom ... Thomas a saint ... his martyrdom is the design of God. Interest focuses within Becket ... the quirks of individuality subordinated to the religious theme – martyrdom is purified by the commitment to the Will of God, thus avoiding the sin of Spiritual Pride. Martyrdom cannot be pursued for the glory of Self – the greatest treason is to do the right thing for the wrong reason.

(b) If martyrdom involves abnegation of the Self, then inevitably Thomas appears as a passive figure: details of his past alluded to, not enacted – drama concentrates on the final days of his life ... the critical moment. The first Three Tempters offer temptations that have already been overcome – sense of inner struggle absent. The Knights assail Thomas, but the outcome is known – no suspense.

(c) Thus we do not find an ebb and flow of events around the hero – in the manner of a Shakespearean historical play. There is no conventional development of character. Struggle/conflict *is* apparent with the Fourth (unexpected) Tempter – but even here the Tempter is a personification of Thomas's inner self. The moment of commitment to God's Will is necessarily hidden – it cannot be dramatized – Thomas withdraws, then re-emerges, his way clear.

(d) If Thomas is a saint, then Eliot has the problem of making him a 'real' man – with the weaknesses of common humanity. Thomas does have a tendency to pontificate – to cultivate his own sainthood, which makes him seem remote, occasionally unattractive. Weaknesses are a point of contact with Shakespeare's tragic heroes – we share them!

(e) Eliot does 'humanize' Becket, none the less: care and concern for the Chorus and Priests; anger (pp. 30–31); courage in the face of his assailants; wistful regret that he cannot enjoy the pleasures of his past and friendship with the King (pp. 47–48). Most, but not all, of these characteristics are compatible with sainthood – and they make us appreciate Becket the man, rather than the abstraction who embodies the martyrdom theme.

(f) *Conclusion*: Becket is characterized as far as is compatible with the theme of the play. He is interesting as a vehicle for the play's religious theme, which is what Eliot intends him to be. It is a play of ideas, to read it with other expectations is misguided. The triumph of the play is that it can engage us in the great issue: what is martyrdom? And the great question: in not seeking to avoid his death, is Becket pursuing his own will, or the Will of God? In the resolution of these questions, Eliot involves us in the redemptive purposes of God for His world. The play, spare and shorn of the conventional 'interests' of the history/chronicle play, enables us to partake of the working-out of God's design without distraction or dilution.

Further reading

Ackroyd, P., *T. S. Eliot* (Hamish Hamilton Ltd., London, 1984) An excellent biography of the poet.

Eliot, T. S., *Poetry and Drama* (Faber & Faber, London, 1950)

A Dialogue on Dramatic Poetry (Faber & Faber, London, 1928)

Gardner, H., *The Art of T. S. Eliot* (Faber & Faber, London, 1949)

Kenner, H., *The Invisible Poet: T. S. Eliot* (Methuen Paperback, London, 1965)

Kenner, H., ed., *T. S. Eliot: Twentieth Century Views* (Prentice-Hall, Englewood Cliffs, N. J. 1962)

Smith, G., *T. S. Eliot's Poetry and Plays* (Univ. of Chicago Press, Chicago, 1956)

Also recommended Nevill Coghill's Introduction and Notes in the *Faber Educational Edition of 'Murder in the Cathedral'* (Faber & Faber, London, 1965).